AF252012

Occidental glorious,
O'er her foes victorious,
Be her praise uproarious,
Occidental fair.

Rarest fellowship is thine,
Love that doth the heart entwine,
Truth and Wisdom's sacred shrine,
Occidental fair.

Here the days glide swiftly by,
Not a shadow in the sky
Till we breathe the parting sigh,
Occidental fair.

To the world's wide bivouac
March thy sons, all cheering back
For the Orange and the Black,
Occidental fair.

'Neath the mountains old and grand,
By the roar of Ocean's strand,
Girt with might forever stand,
Occidental fair.

*(Composed in 1908, with words by professor of classics
William Dennis Ward, and music by Ethel Ward Johnson)*

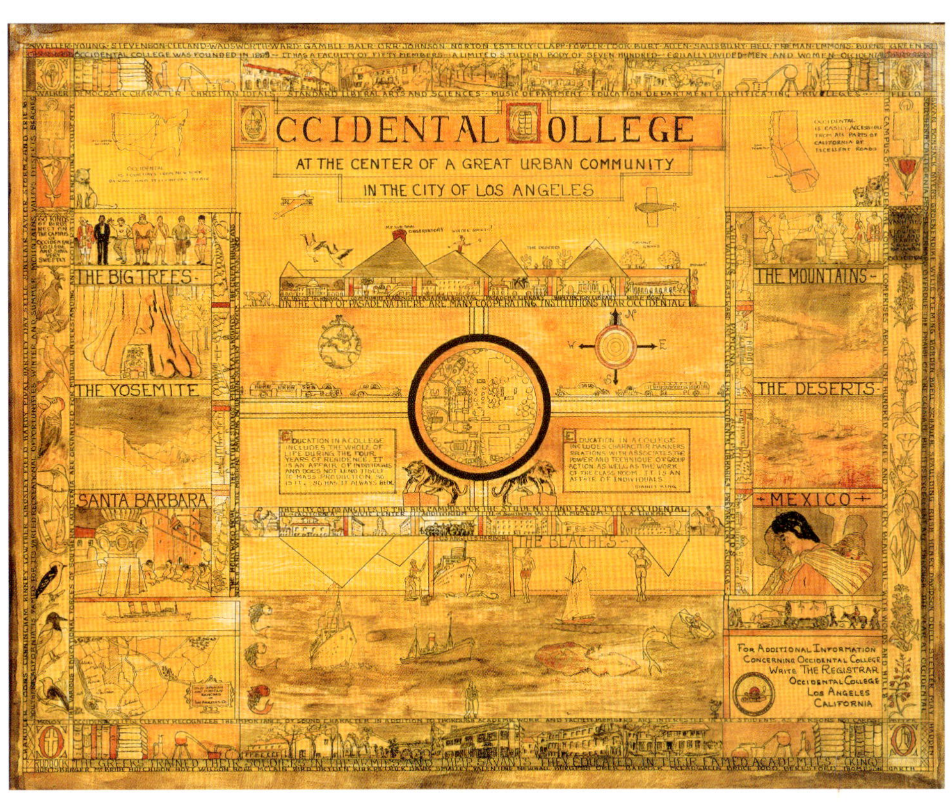

OCCIDENTAL
FAIR

The Booksmith Group

PUBLISHER
Stephen D. Giddens

PUBLISHING CONSULTANT
Leeanne Seely

PHOTO EDITOR
Bobby Sagmiller
VisibilityCreative.com

TEXT
Kim O'Connor

INTERIOR TEMPLATE DESIGN
Roy Roper, wideyedesign

Occidental College

DIRECTOR OF COMMUNICATIONS
Jim Tranquada

PUBLICATIONS EDITOR
Dick Anderson

DIRECTOR OF ALUMNI RELATIONS
James Jacobs

COLLEGE ARCHIVIST
Jean Paule

PHOTOGRAPHY
Kevin Burke
David Gautreau
Max S. Gerber
Kirby Lee
Glenn Mar '84
Kyna Shilling '06
Special Collections

©2008 BY THE BOOKSMITH GROUP
All rights reserved. No part of this publication may be reproduced in any form or by
any means, electronic or mechanical, including photocopying and recording, or by any
information storage or retrieval system, without prior written permission from the publisher.

Published in the United States of America by
The Booksmith Group, an imprint of FRP
a wholly owned subsidiary of Southwestern/Great American, Inc.
P. O. Box 305124
Nashville, TN 37230
1-800-358-0560
www.thebooksmithgroup.com

ISBN (Standard): 978-1-934892-17-6
Library of Congress Control Number: 2008931981

Printed in the United States of America
First printing 2008

This book is dedicated to Jean Paule—
honorary member of the Class of 2005,
valued assistant to Presidents Coons and Gilman,
volunteer College archivist since 1996,
and an irreplaceable treasure
in Occidental's Special Collections

Introduction
4

Chapter 1
Occidental
Glorious
10

Chapter 2
Io Triumphe!
36

Chapter 3
Praise
Uproarious
66

Chapter 4
O'er her foes
Victorious
94

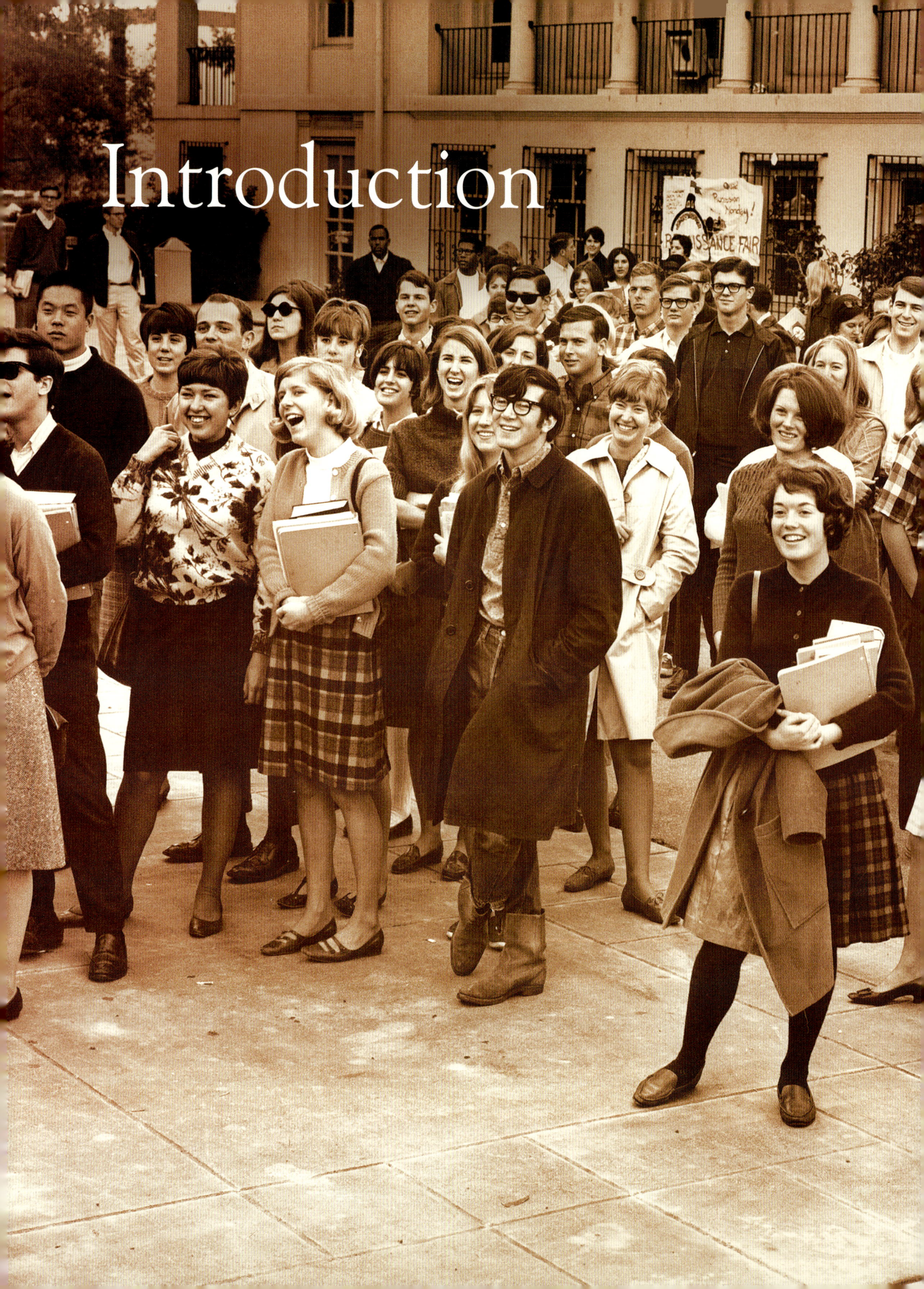

Introduction

hose who have visited Occidental College know something about the power of love at first sight. As a senior in high school, Suzo McKellar '58 climbed on a bus with her peers to visit local college prospects. Upon arriving at Eagle Rock, she was immediately struck by the hospitality of Occidental College. "We went to Pomona, and I thought it was a fabulous campus with a wonderful library," she recalls. "When we went to Oxy the next week, the school had all the kids who had gone to our high school greet us at the bus. All of the sudden, Oxy seemed so friendly.

"That was merchandising! Of the 26 people on the bus, 23 went to Oxy."

A gathering of students enjoys the off-camera antics of auctioneer Bob Winter, associate professor of the history of civilization, during Renaissance Week in 1967. The weeklong observance included an auction of student and faculty art to aid the restoration of Italian art damaged in the Florence Flood of 1966.

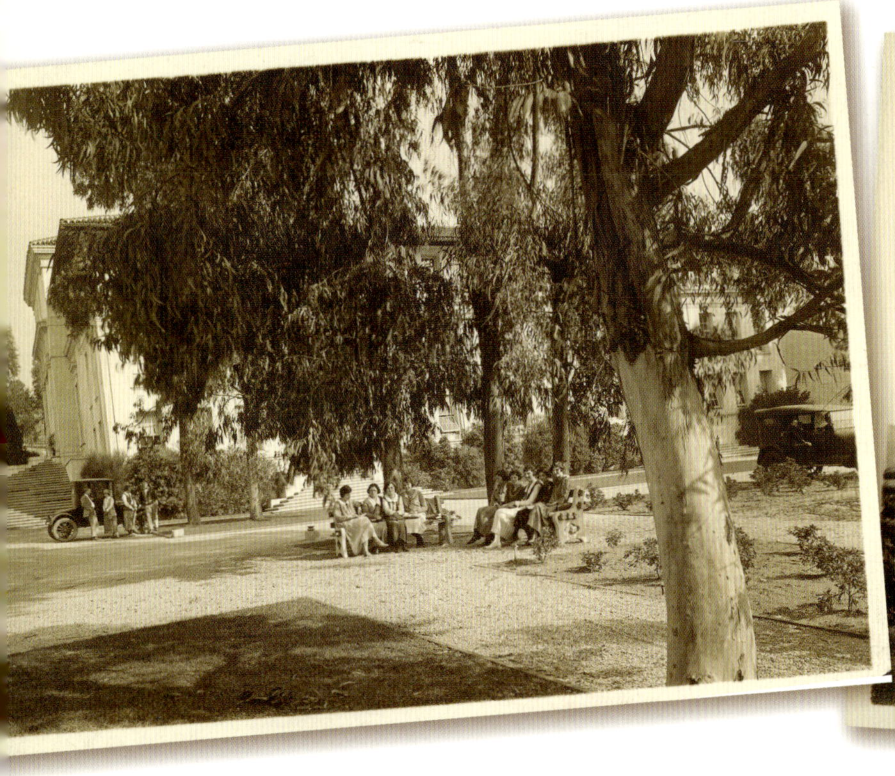

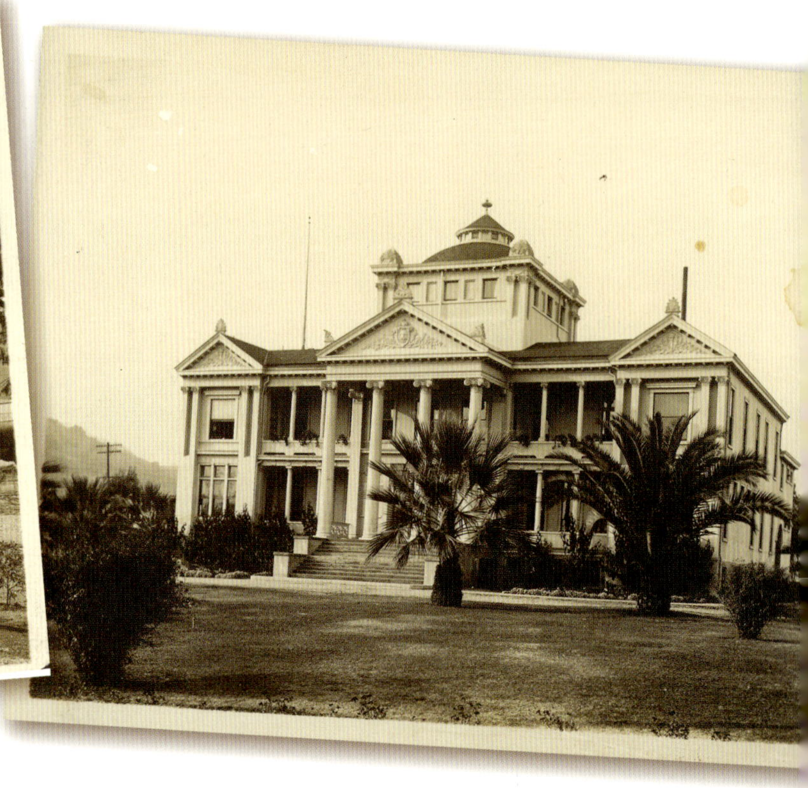

ABOVE LEFT: *The Occidental campus, circa 1927.*

ABOVE RIGHT: *The Academy Building on Occidental's Highland Park campus, home to the College from 1898-1914.*

BELOW: *Architect Myron Hunt surveys the future site of Oxy's Eagle Rock campus, circa 1910.*

Almost anyone who has spent time at Oxy shares a similar story—a visceral moment when they were deeply stirred by a college they did not yet know. It is easy to see why. The campus is beautiful, enhanced by the careful attention of generations of planners and caretakers. Yet, while so many are first taken in by what the school offers the eye, they are more moved by what it offers the head and the heart.

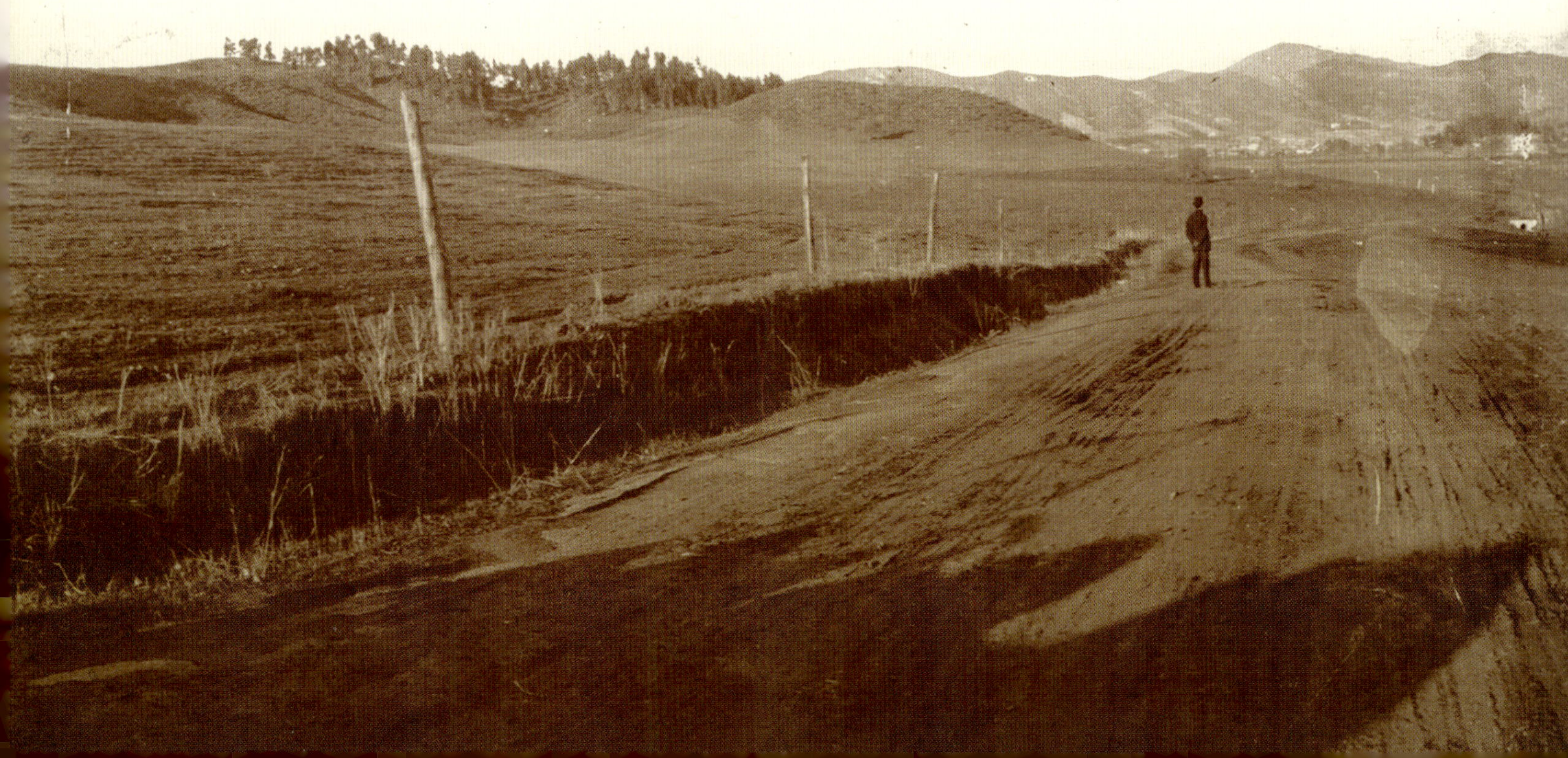

Just as the face of campus has evolved—building on Myron Hunt's original design by repurposing old buildings and adding new facilities—so has an Occidental education. From the beginning, Oxy has offered a strong liberal arts education in an inclusive environment. That tradition remains important; the school has had effective leaders that were committed to the institution's original vision while being creative enough to reinterpret it.

"I think that one of the things about the College is that each of its presidents drew on pieces of Occidental's heritage and emphasized them," says Ted Mitchell, Occidental's twelfth president (1999-2005). "I don't think that I invented financial security, nor did John Slaughter (Oxy's eleventh president, 1989-1998) invent diversity. The College has been committed to diversity from its beginning. The College has been committed to creating strong, vibrant, academic programs from its beginning. We all grew from each other and learned from each other. We all stood on each other's shoulders."

These pages are a tribute to all that Occidental College was, all that it is, and all that it will become. A strong liberal arts education and an enduring affection for Oxy tie today's students to the 300 or so young people who first populated the Eagle Rock campus. It is the kind of nostalgia that endures long past graduation.

"I always come back to the campus when I am down," says Jim Cerveny '61. "I just jump in the car and drive here. I get out and I walk around this campus. I walk on the track and feel like the Energizer bunny. I realize that when I leave, I'm still going to have the same problem. But I'm ready to go because I'm not afraid to work on finding a solution and keep going."

It is also a nostalgia that transcends the boundaries of campus. "It's still a wonderful thing for me to be able to walk down the streets of San Francisco or Boston and all of a sudden catch the eye of one of my former students," says Mitchell. "We're able to pick up right up where we left off. The relationships are magical and they persist over a lifetime."

Alumni returning to Oxy today would be amazed at both how much—and how little—the campus has changed over time. "What lasts and what binds us together is the unseen and never-to-be-seen," the late Lawrence Clark Powell '28 once observed. "It is the very essence of education—the enrichment of the mind with learning and of the heart with affection."

Occidental Glorious

In the fall of 1948 freshmen filed into Thorne Hall for the first meeting of History of Civilization, an epic course in every sense.

It didn't take long for "Civ" to become an institution, but it started as a collaborative experiment. Mindful of trends in higher education, President Arthur G. Coons '20 initiated a course developed by Dean Robert E. Fitch and the faculty that mirrored interdisciplinary programs that were springing up at schools like the University of Chicago. The first version was launched in 1947, gathering perspectives from faculty in the social sciences and the humanities under the umbrella of a single class.

ABOVE: *Traveling by camel "at the average rate of two miles an hour hardly enhances the monotony of the desert scene," associate professor of religion Silva Lake once told a journalist, "but it is conducive to study."*

That course quickly evolved into History of Civilization, which drew on the expertise of departments as diverse as history, political science, economics, sociology, philosophy, religion, psychology, literature, music, and art. Freshmen and sophomores were exposed to a dizzying array of professors as they walked through the Western world's major achievements from the Greeks to the moderns. A lecture about political science by Raymond McKelvey might be followed by a lecture about religion by Biblical archeologist Silva Lake. Laurence de Rycke explained economics and Bob Winter taught architecture. "It started out with theories of evolution," recalls one alumnus, "and took you marching across the world."

At the same time, the course was a social experiment, as frequent lectures, discussion groups, and late nights with the assigned reading at the library turned strangers into colleagues. "It created a sense of unity because we all had the same experience," says Ann Moyes '53.

Oxy revamped its curriculum in the early 1970s to reflect the changing world and, along with it, the expanding scope of academic inquiry. Students and faculty were no longer content to focus their studies on the Western world. History of Civilization, ironically, was a casualty of progress.

"The two-year sequence simply couldn't accommodate all of the fields that the students and faculty were becoming interested in," says former President Richard Gilman, who oversaw the evolution of the curriculum. "A program that characterized the College over many student generations was no longer considered adequate for the new interests, opportunities, and emphases that were developing."

While this development was met ruefully by many alumni who looked back fondly at their collective time in Thorne Hall, Gilman adds: "If you talk to students from recent years, many of them will say that the most important part of their education was working closely on some advanced topic or special interest with the faculty. Specialization and compartmentalization is part of the fabric of intellectual change. It was a necessary response to the changes in our academic environment."

LEFT: Professors Raymond McKelvey (political science) and Joseph Haring (economics) engage in the decades-old practice of Quad-sitting at lunchtime in this 1970 photo.

BELOW: In his 40-year tenure at Occidental (1962-2002), professor of anthropology C. Scott Littleton lectured frequently on Japanese myth and religion, Arthurian and Holy Grail legends, and the theories of the late French mythologist Georges Dumézil.

OPPOSITE: Occidental faculty members share a good book in this 1956 photo: (back row) Laurence de Rycke (economics), John Rodes (history of civilization), Raymond Lindgren (history); (front row) Paul Sheldon (sociology), Kenneth Oliver (English and comparative literature), and Andrew Rolle '43 (history).

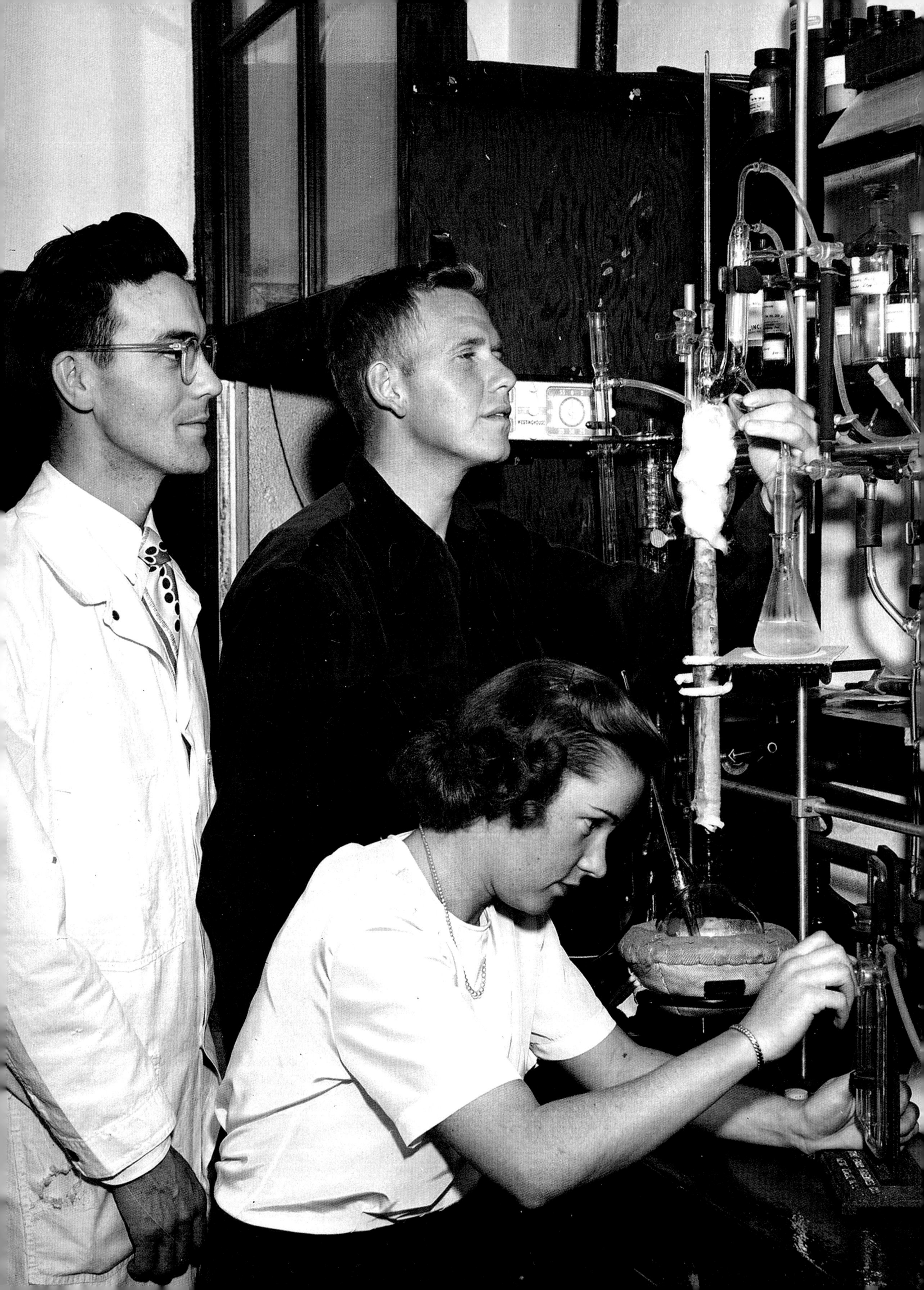

History of Civilization met for the last time in 1970, but the course, like the Occidental experience itself, has left an indelible mark on its students. Even now, alumni will tell you that those Thorne Hall lectures, absorbed more than 30 years ago, enhance their lives in unexpected ways. "The class really comes in handy now," says Jim Cerveny '61. "I went to Italy in 2005 for the first time. All the things that I remembered from class about wars and gladiators were coming to life."

Yet Civ imparted something more than the mere ability to recognize ancient monuments; it encouraged students to stay curious and critical wherever they found themselves. "My husband and I still comment on how valuable the course was," says Ginny Cushman '55. "We travel and see paintings that we studied; we recognize them. We have always said that Oxy fills you with a desire to never stop learning."

As it turned out, that desire was not just a product of History of Civilization. A deep love of learning will long outlast the curricula of yesterday, today, or tomorrow; it is the very essence of what it means to have an Oxy education.

ABOVE: Associate professor of religion Margery Freeman introduced Marriage and the Family into the Oxy curriculum in 1941. Students commonly referred to the evening class as "Sex at 7."

OPPOSITE: Frank Lambert joined the chemistry department in 1948, becoming a full professor in 1956. He helped develop the College's summer student research program and today has five well-trafficked websites devoted to the thermodynamics concept of entropy.

SPOTLIGHT

Andrew Rolle
PROFESSOR OF AMERICAN HISTORY

As a student and longtime professor, Andrew Rolle '43 has watched Occidental College evolve with the keen eye of a historian. Though he has dedicated two volumes (published in 1962 and 1987) to documenting and analyzing the institution's transformation, he himself has changed very little.

Rolle barely had a moment to himself as an undergraduate. In fact, he held down more jobs during his college years than some people have in an entire lifetime. He earned 25 cents an hour as an employee of the library. He mowed lawns and worked in a meatpacking plant (a job that was especially hard on his roommate, who often woke in the middle of the night to the grisly sight of a blood-soaked Rolle). He even packed students into his 1932 Chevrolet, running a taxi service from the campus into Pasadena—15 cents one way, a round-trip for a quarter.

His work ethic carried over into the classroom. A self-described "nerd," Rolle spent all of his free time with his books. His excellent GPA made up for his rather lackluster social life. There was hardly time for dancing when he had so much to learn.

After graduation, the war took him to Europe, where his Occidental education literally saved him from drowning; Rolle, a land lover, had been required to learn the sidestroke in order to graduate. After a brief career in the Foreign Service, he returned stateside for his Ph.D. He was back at Occidental less than a decade after he graduated, joining the faculty in 1952.

Initially, the young teacher found his alma mater virtually unchanged. Students still dressed for dinner, as they had in his day, but it wasn't long before those formalities fell away during the upheaval of the '60s. "Everything was going fine until the 1960s," Rolle says. "All of a sudden, they wanted to call me 'Andy baby.' I didn't want to be called 'Andy baby.' I wanted to be called 'Professor.' I worked hard to earn that title!"

In defiance of the times, the world remained static within the walls of Rolle's classroom. His reputation as tough-but-fair stuck through his tenure of 36 years. "People wouldn't take my classes unless they really wanted to work," he says. "I gave them a lot for their money."

These days, Rolle still keeps an eye on the College, though he has "retired" to a position at Huntington Library. Some old habits die hard.

ABOVE: *Rolle (shown in a 2004 photo) walks most days from his San Marino home to the nearby Huntington Library, where he has been a senior scholar since 1989.*

OPPOSITE: *Rolle discusses U.S. history with Eqbal Ahmad, an exchange student from Forman Christian College in Pakistan during the 1957-58 academic year.*

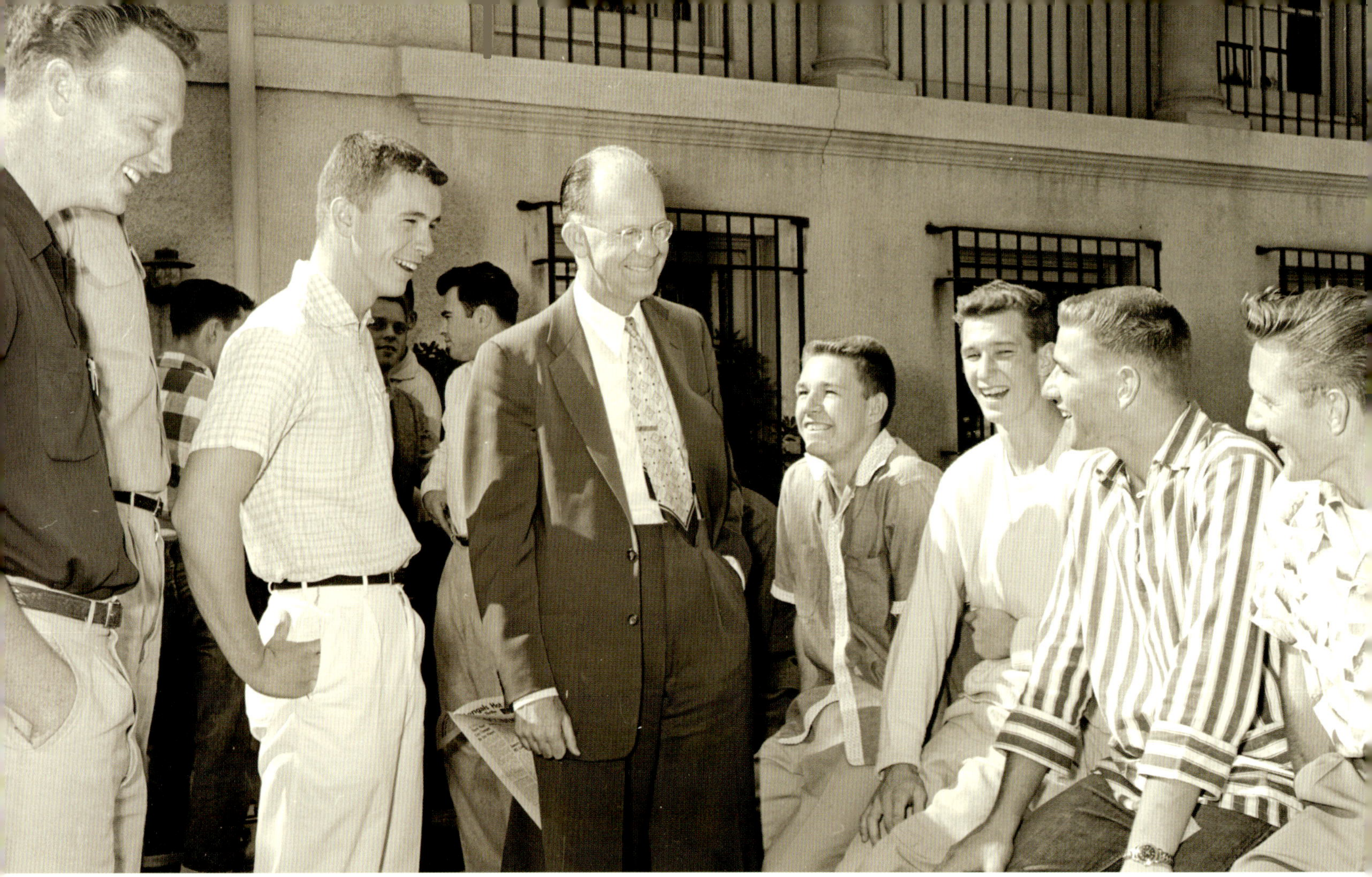

ABOVE: *Ben Culley (in a 1955 photo) joined Oxy's mathematics department in 1943 but often served the College in dual capacities, including dean of men, dean of students, and director of financial aid. "You were truly a Renaissance man in your interests in both the mind and in the body," Allen Gresham '53 noted at a memorial service for Culley in 1982.*

BELOW: *Donald Loftsgordon (second from right, with Cyril Gloyn '27, Silva Lake, and Keith Beebe '43 of the philosophy department) taught at Oxy from 1960 until his death at age 39 in 1966. An award for outstanding teaching, established by the ASOC in Loftsgordon's memory, is voted on by the senior class each spring.*

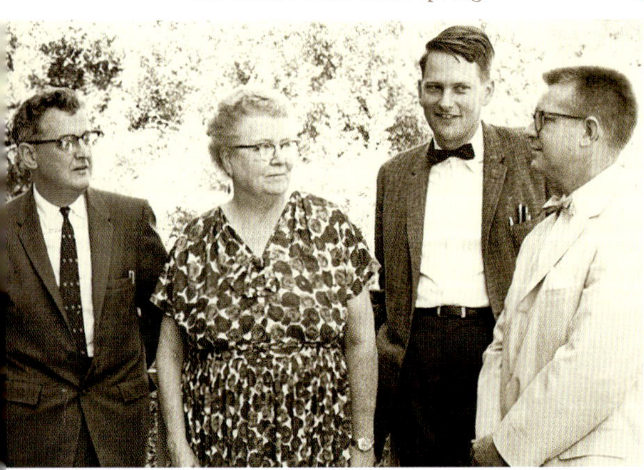

Houston: We Have a Problem

Occidental has never had a reputation of being an easy "A." And much of the credit—or the blame—for that can be traced back to a single person: Percy Houston, professor of English.

"It was Percy Houston who introduced us to the grading system at the College," Addie (Grant) McMenamin '40 says. "According to him, to get an A, you have to have an inner gift. For a B, you need mechanical correctness and a sense of style. Anyone can earn a C. D is a grade we give when it should be an F, but we need you to keep coming back to pay tuition."

The late author, librarian, and bibliographer Lawrence Clark Powell '28—no slouch in the writing department—recalled the following in 1978: "As an undergraduate, I was a bad writer. Professor Houston told me so. I'm afraid it didn't sink in. I kept on writing—badly. The last time I saw Percy Houston, I had just published a book. I'd sent him a copy, seeking his approval. What did I get? 'Larry,' he said, 'I can say this about you: You are persistent.'"

ABOVE: John McMenamin '40 (with students in the early 1950s) was hired as the fourth person in Occidental's biology department in the first expansion of the faculty after the Second World War.

LEFT: Arthur G. Coons '20 (shown in 1962) became Occidental's ninth president in 1946, shepherding the College through nearly 20 years of curricular advancements, campus improvements, and endowment growth following World War II.

A Collaborative Campus

Occidental has long cultivated a unique and decidedly collaborative environment between faculty and student. Professors not only trust, but depend on, students to help perform research, collect data, and even co-author papers. Such an arrangement goes by another name at most institutions: graduate school. The deliberate recruitment of professionally active faculty was an initiative of Gilman's when he came to the College in 1965.

"Here was an institution that was ready to move in directions that I thought were important," he recalls. Gilman did not set out to create a "publish or perish" environment, but to make sure that students were exposed to creative research. It followed that if faculty remained engaged in their fields, they would have an easier job of engaging their students.

It was a decision based on the pioneering work of faculty in the biology and chemistry departments during the previous decade. Building on the leadership of several Occidental scientists who helped found the Council on Undergraduate Research in the early 1980s, a 1987 Ford Foundation grant made it possible to extend research opportunities to other disciplines, especially the social sciences.

ABOVE: Accompanied by chemistry professor and dean of students John McAnally and President Richard Gilman, civil rights leader Martin Luther King Jr. greets a student following his standing-room-only speech in Thorne Hall on April 12, 1967.

OPPOSITE, TOP: Professor of mathematics Joan Rand Moschovakis taught at Occidental from 1965 to 1995. Her most popular course? Introduction to Topology.

OPPOSITE, BOTTOM: Students line up inside Alumni Gymnasium to register for spring courses in March 1967.

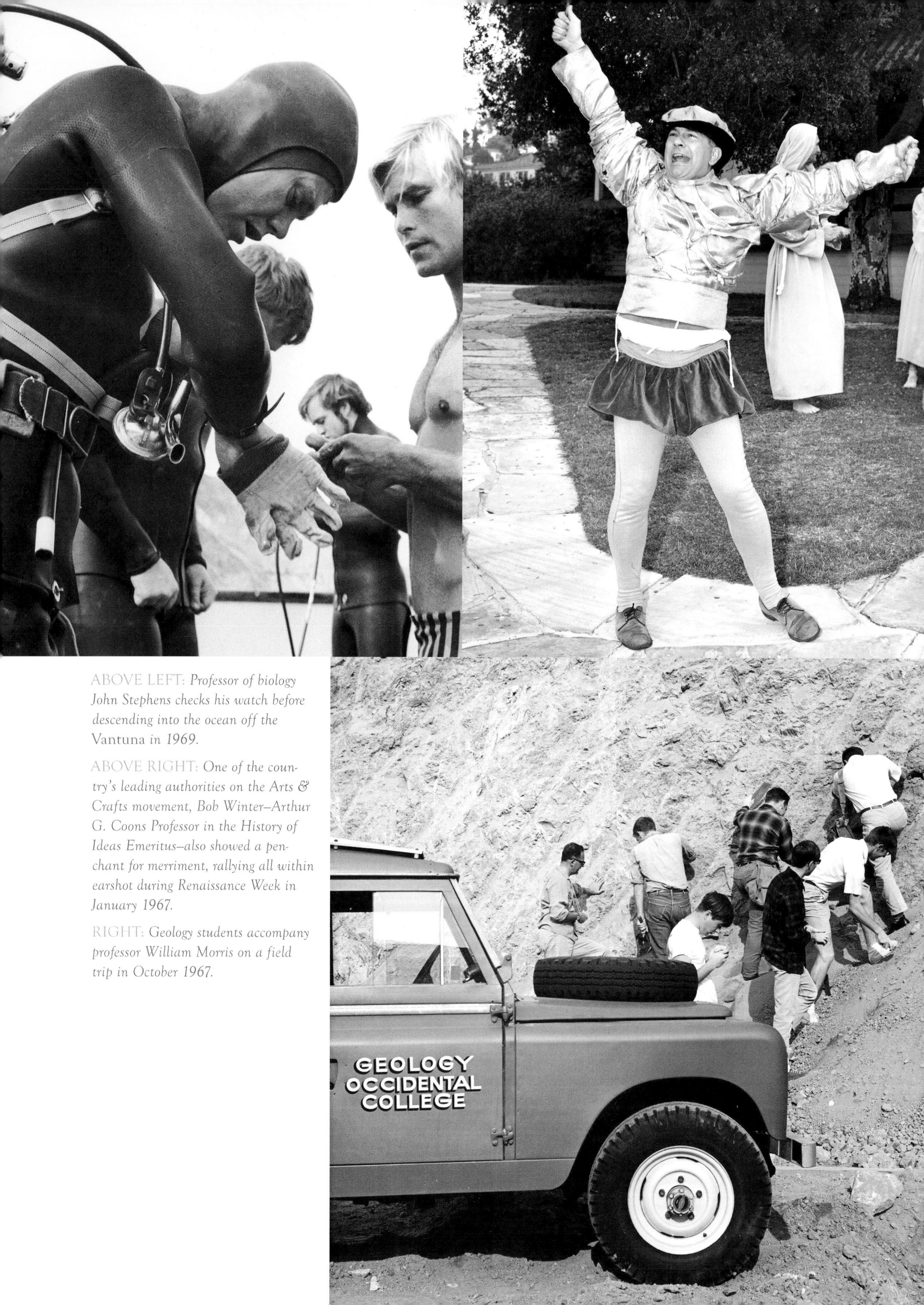

ABOVE LEFT: *Professor of biology John Stephens checks his watch before descending into the ocean off the Vantuna in 1969.*

ABOVE RIGHT: *One of the country's leading authorities on the Arts & Crafts movement, Bob Winter—Arthur G. Coons Professor in the History of Ideas Emeritus—also showed a penchant for merriment, rallying all within earshot during Renaissance Week in January 1967.*

RIGHT: *Geology students accompany professor William Morris on a field trip in October 1967.*

Ten years later, the College received one of 10 awards for the Integration of Research and Education from the National Science Foundation that established the Undergraduate Research Center. Each year, more than 250 students work with faculty on original research in a wide range of fields.

"The faculty is remarkable for the breadth of its strength," former President Ted Mitchell observes. "Oxy has always prided itself on having very professional faculty. It creates a venue for liberal arts teaching that is more than just classroom instruction. It is based on real, original inquiry."

President Richard C. Gilman signs matriculation parchments for the 453 newly arrived members of the Class of '74. Gilman initiated the tradition, which continues today, of personally greeting each member of the entering class during his or her first week on campus—a practice he borrowed from his undergraduate experience at Dartmouth.

SPOTLIGHT

Laurence de Rycke
PROFESSOR OF ECONOMICS

A "hard-headed Dutchman" by his own admission, Laurence de Rycke was said to make the best martini "this side of the Stork Club" and offered many pearls of wisdom to his students, including the following: "You can have the knowledge of the angels but if you can't express it you're dead." "If you're going to cheat, that's up to you. But don't ever cheat the IRS." And finally, "Better to be at the foot of a great teacher than a thousand feet from a great name."

Laurence de Rycke came to Occidental in 1943 having worked at the Department of State, where he was known as an authority on international economics and banking. He immediately became known for his astonishing ability to transform the most immature freshman into a young professional ready for anything the business world could throw her way.

His standards were high—some might say outrageously high—but he knew how to get results. John Wright '49 had been under fire in Europe in World War II and thought he'd never be so scared again—until he took de Rycke's course on Money and Banking. "Nothing could be as intimidating as the 88, that famous German anti-aircraft, anti-tank, anti-personnel, anti-ambulance field piece, but Dr. de Rycke came close," Wright recalls. "There's no question about it—he totally changed my life," says Glenn Weirick '58. "He taught you how to write clearly, succinctly, and to the point. He was very exacting in what he expected of you."

De Rycke was also a character in his own right. "He was impeccable," says Brenda Hill '71. "He had a black suit and a heavily starched white shirt with a monogram on it—very rigid. The first day of class, he would tell you that he was susceptible to germs. If you coughed once, back of the room. If you coughed twice, you had to leave and couldn't come back without a doctor's permission slip.

"He was merciless," she adds, "but he just knew economics so well."

"A *Fang* magazine poll said three things about Dr. de Rycke," Wright says. "First, he was the best dressed member of the faculty. Second, he was the best teacher at Oxy. Third, he was the worst slave driver at Oxy. I absolutely agree with all three."

"Some faculty members have told me that students' ideas have actually shaped their research agendas," says former President Susan Prager (2006-2007). "Geology professor Jim Sadd, who is well known for his work using global positioning systems to study the distribution of environmental hazards, said the idea for that research came to him from a group of students."

As Gilman and the faculty pursued the development of undergraduate research, Occidental was growing in other important ways. The 1960s ushered in an era of expansion, with Oxy deepening its engagement with the community through projects such as the Community Literacy Center. The Center was established in 1963 as a speech and reading clinic, but it has evolved into a two-credit course for Occidental students who work one-on-one with local elementary school students in creative tutoring sessions that involve everything from reading books to performing plays.

TOP: Jane Jaquette, Bertha Harton Orr Professor of Politics Emerita, has published widely on women in politics in Latin America. She joined the Occidental faculty in 1969.

ABOVE: Larry Caldwell, Cecil H. and Louise Gamble Professor of Politics, came to Oxy in 1967 and is on course to be the College's longest-serving faculty member.

SPOTLIGHT

Joe Birman
PROFESSOR OF GEOLOGY

Professor Joe Birman, below right, examines a geological specimen with colleague David Cummings in 1971. "Professor Birman was my early guiding light," Eleanor F. Helin '54—a planetary scientist and astronomer with Jet Propulsion Laboratory—wrote in 1998. "His enthusiasm, love of his subject matter, and personality served as an outstanding motivator. He opened the door to geology and some early comparative solar system science." Above, an apple tree descended from Sir Isaac Newton's estate grows outside Herrick Interfaith Center—the fruit of Birman's travels.

Joe Birman had an awfully long career at Occidental for someone who didn't even intend to work as a college professor.

He came to Oxy in 1950 to take over the geology department after its head was called away to serve in the Korean War. Over the 30-plus years taught here, he proved himself to be an innovator (he pioneered a technique that uses ground temperature to find underground water) and a favorite teacher among students.

There is no doubt that part of his popularity was due to his rather wicked sense of humor. Birman famously led his students, equipment in hand, into the Quad on a hunt for uranium to celebrate April 1, 1955. He is, perhaps, less known for his poetry. "In the late '60s or early '70s, I began writing limericks about the faculty," he says. "The criteria were that in the first place the limerick was clean, and secondly that I would only write them for tenured faculty."

Consider this limerick, never before published, on longtime biology professor John McMenamin '40:

Intent upon learning the worst:
"Did the egg or the chicken come first?"
John McMenamin's yen
Was to query a hen.
What a strong intellectual thirst!

But his most enduring contribution to Occidental is in the unlikely form of an apple tree on the south side of Herrick Interfaith Center. Birman and his wife, Barbara, were visiting England when they stumbled upon Sir Isaac Newton's house during a drive to London. "We wandered around the house and there was very little," he says, "but there was a lawn with three gnarled apple trees. I picked two apples and put one in my jacket pocket. I brought it back to the biology department. They somehow germinated and planted the seeds, so now Occidental has an apple tree from Isaac Newton's estate."

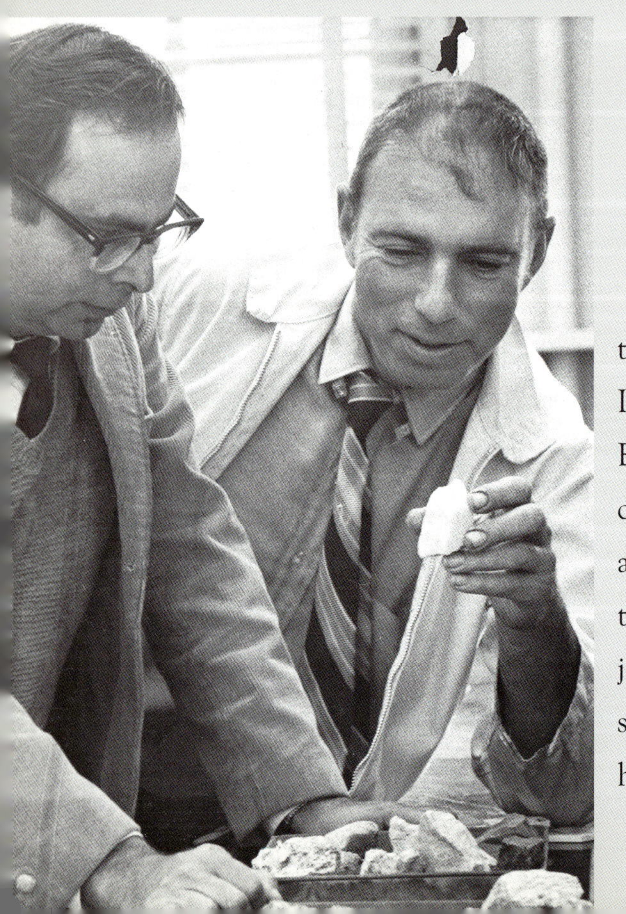

Soon thereafter, Occidental became one of the nation's first institutions of higher learning to offer an Upward Bound program when it joined the federal pilot program and offered its first courses in 1966. It has offered programming to local high school students ever since. During the school year, Oxy students serve as advisors to at-risk youth; in the summers, the College hosts an intensive program where high schoolers live on campus for five weeks.

Susan Madrid-Simon, who has served as the program's director since 1990, feels that Oxy's Upward Bound chapter is unique in that it is so well integrated with the school. "We are a really rare program," she says. "You can go to other campuses and you really know that Upward Bound is the stepchild division. That is not the case here, and that really enables us to make real commitments to local schools that we know we can follow through on."

TOP: *Arthur G. Coons Professor in the History of Ideas Roger Boesche (shown in a 1986 photo) gained national media attention after a Los Angeles* Times *profile of presidential candidate and U.S. Sen. Barack Obama '83 described him as "Obama's intellectual mentor" at Oxy.*

ABOVE: *As an undergraduate at Oxy, "I was clearly heading toward the humanities," recalls Eric Newhall '67, professor of English and comparative literary studies. He ultimately chose to major in English, he says, because "I simply liked great novels a little bit more."*

LEFT: *A.H. "Woody" Studenmund joined the Occidental faculty in 1970. In addition to being Richard W. Millar Professor of Economics and Finance and chair of the economics department, he is the author of* Using Econometrics: A Practical Guide.

Context and Community

Diversity has been incorporated into the Occidental model
since its inception. Occidental's first graduates in 1893, Maude
Bell and Martha Thompson, were women. Pedro Recio, Oxy's
first Latino graduate, received his degree four years later. Soon
Ki Rhee Lee, the College's first Asian graduate, was a member
of the Class of 1910. "Oxy was one of the early coeducational
institutions in the country," former President Ted Mitchell
points out. "That decision was pathbreaking."

The College's commitment to equal-opportunity education extended from its efforts to aid Japanese students confined
to internment camps during World War II through President
Coons's tenure, when Baltimore Scott '62 became the first
African-American president of Oxy's student government.
Under President John Brooks Slaughter, the College adopted
a new mission statement, *Of Excellence and Equity*, and took
major strides toward diversifying the student body by attracting
greater numbers of outstanding students of color.

Occidental's desire to connect with and learn from the community set an important precedent. When Mitchell came to Oxy in 1999, he knew that Oxy had to look for new ways to connect students to the world around them. "We had to really rethink what it meant to be liberally educated in the 21st century," he says. Led by the faculty, the curriculum became increasingly interdisciplinary, participation in study abroad programs grew rapidly, and the College found creative ways to take advantage of the myriad learning opportunities that the region has to offer.

One result of this approach was the Center for Community Based Learning. "It was a real innovation for the College," Mitchell says. "It was quite explicitly designed to connect theoretical and practical approaches to learning and to help students give back both in the sense of volunteerism, but also in the sense of connecting the learning that they are doing with learning in the community."

ABOVE: *Ted Mitchell served as Occidental's 12th president from 1999 to 2005—a six-year tenure marked by dramatic increases in applications, fundraising, and national reputation for the College.*

LEFT: *Associate professor Daniel Snowden-Ifft, who joined the physics department in 1997, works on his detector beneath 300 feet of concrete in the Morris Dam above Azusa in 2000. The detector is used to discover dark matter, thought to make up most of the universe's mass.*

OPPOSITE TOP: *"The business we are in is teacher training," says associate professor of education Ron Solórzano, a member of the Occidental faculty since 1994 as well as an accomplished guitarist with the 10-person band Mestizo.*

OPPOSITE BOTTOM: *A seasoned educator admired for his skills as a mediator, negotiator, and cultural ambassador, John Brooks Slaughter came to Oxy in 1988 with the goal of providing "a gifted and diverse group of students with a total educational experience of the highest quality."*

Overseas study and an international orientation among the faculty have a long history at Occidental, dating back to the College's historic Presbyterian roots. As early as 1910, almost 10 percent of alumni had foreign addresses, nearly all reflecting missionary service. In 1916, the College entered into its first overseas study program with Hangchow Christian College in which a graduating senior spent a year in China as an instructor. Occidental's first international exchange program began in 1935 with Lingnan University, also in China. It wasn't until the 1969-70 academic year that the overseas study program as it's known today was launched when 10 juniors were officially enrolled at the Universität des Saarlandes in Germany. The program has grown steadily since then; in the 2006-07 academic year, 172 students, or 41 percent of the junior class, went overseas.

It was in 1919 that the Norman Bridge Professorship in Hispanic American History was endowed; the first incumbent, Robert Glass Cleland, Class of 1907, taught courses on Mexico and Latin America. The appointment of other faculty with international interests soon followed, most notably John Parke Young '17 and Arthur G. Coons '20 in economics. It was on this foundation that the Stuart Chevalier Program in Diplomacy and World Affairs was endowed in 1957, an interdisciplinary program designed to prepare students for a wide range of careers.

Since 1986 the College has offered Occidental-at-the-United Nations, the only undergraduate program in the country to offer internships in a variety of departments in the United Nations secretariat, in addition to the U.S. Mission to the United Nations.

Since the 1990s, a number of service-learning programs (both formal and informal) have found exciting new ways to broaden and deepen what it means to earn an Oxy education. Chris Craney, chemistry professor and founder of a successful outreach program called Teachers + Occidental = Partnership in Science, points out that the College has become a model as other institutions reconsider what a liberal arts education should be. "Our accomplishments are especially impressive when you consider that this is a pretty small place," he says. "Lots of schools are trying to replicate the things we've done here at Oxy."

ABOVE: Physics professor Dennis Eggleston (center, with undergraduate assistants Alexandra Kearns '10 and Joshua Williams '08) performs experimental research on plasmas, the charged gases sometimes referred to as the fourth state of matter.

OPPOSITE: Professor Wellington Chan joined the Occidental history department in 1971 and has published extensively on the socioeconomic history of modern and contemporary China. He also modeled Oxy Wear for the magazine in 2003.

A Bird's-Eye View of Oxy
THE DRAWINGS OF REMSEN D. BIRD

"When I concentrate, I doodle!" Remsen D. Bird—Occidental's eighth and longest-serving president (1921-1946)—once observed. And when Bird and his wife, Helen, retired to Carmel in 1946, he burned all but four of the notebooks whose pages he had filled while at Oxy. If only we could turn back time.

Those that remained—and other sketchbooks from later years—wound up in the hands of Occidental in the 1960s, thanks largely to the efforts of Patricia (Henry) Yeomans '38, who collected some 500 of Bird's caricatures for sale (for the bargain price of $1 apiece) by the Occidental College Women's Club boutique to raise money for scholarships.

Whether the subject is work, food, the world at large, or his beloved dog, Meg, Bird brought a whimsical flare to many of his drawings. He was often his own best subject, and his observations about the presidency—the subject of an entire 28-page black-and-white booklet—are timeless. We could fill an entire chapter with our favorite Birds, but for now, enjoy these watercolor gems from a leader whose artistic legacy endures.

ABOVE LEFT: *Pressing the flesh with Helen at his side: "I do not think my best contribution was raising money or making friends for the College," Bird observed in 1963. "I think it was in the keeping of the basic purposes of the College—the freedom to search, teach, and express opinions."*

ABOVE: *Bird tosses and turns during the night, top—maybe because of something he ate?*

CHAPTER TWO
Io
Triumphe!

In the fall of 1951, as students milled about the Quad, celebrating the start of another school year, even the most casual observer could easily discern the freshmen among the lot—just by looking at their heads.

The dink, also known as a freshman cap or a beanie, originally came in orange and black, though it was later offered in a fetching shade of green. Dinks were issued to all Oxy freshmen, who were obligated to sport them for the first few weeks of their academic careers—a practice that stretched from the first years of the 20th century well into the 1950s.

As if that wasn't enough to mark the freshmen, you would have been hard-pressed to miss the oversized signs they wore on their backs.

Freshmen from the Class of '55 grapple with sophomore members of the Class of '54 in a ball-pushing competition— a variation on tug-of-war and one of many Orientation games of the era.

ABOVE: *Arthur Westerfield '21, left, and James Sheppard '21 make the dash to class in this 1917 photo.*

BELOW: *Freshman-sophomore mud-fights (such as this 1951 melee in the muck) were a staple of the Orientation experience until Oxy cleaned up its act.*

OPPOSITE: *One of the three original buildings on campus, Fowler Hall was completed in 1914. It was renovated in 2005.*

Facebook had nothing on these young men and women, whose names were displayed in large letters on the handmade posters. Students were required to gather signatures from upper-classmen, a rule that was strictly—though cheerfully—enforced.

Those were just a few of the good-natured edicts passed down by the sophomores who had endured the same humiliations when they arrived at Oxy. "Remember how in those days we had to hop on one foot across the Quad between Johnson and Fowler halls?" Rev. Fred Appleton '30 recalled on the occasion of his class's golden anniversary. "And wear those funny little beanies, and not get caught talking to girls, and never go through a door ahead of a sophomore or upperclassman? It was a little like joining the Marines or going to prison."

In the 1940s, freshmen were given an orange-and-black poodle toy that would be their charge for the entire year. And for many decades, freshmen were formally quizzed to make sure they had learned "Io Triumphe," the College's enduring cheer.

And while the thought of gathering signatures for a poster while wearing a dink or caring for a stuffed animal might sound mortifying to the modern student, this mild-mannered hazing had at least one thing going for it: It made meeting people awfully easy.

FOWLER
HALL

Fashions, Passions, and Vision

ABOVE: *Architect Myron Hunt, who once shared an office with Frank Lloyd Wright, recognized the value of inspiring students through their surroundings.*

OPPOSITE, TOP: *Open your mouth and say "Ahhhh": Ruby Rich Burgar, head nurse in Emmons Health Center from 1943 to 1974, examines Oxy scholar-athletes in a 1945 photo.*

OPPOSITE, BOTTOM: *A typical women's dormitory room in 1940. A typical residence life dilemma of the era was "too many females and too few telephones," recalls Mickey (Wallace) Wheat '46. "For outgoing calls you had to have 5 cents ready, and nickels were always in short supply. Barbara Carter '46 cleverly saved tips from a summer job in Yosemite and loaned nickels to frantic dorm friends—for a price."*

Campus life has changed considerably since Occidental's Eagle Rock campus was dedicated in 1914. The very face of Oxy evolved steadily through the first half of the 20th century, beginning with the first three structures built by architect Myron Hunt—Johnson for the liberal arts, Fowler for the sciences, and Swan for a men's dormitory. By the time Hunt retired in 1940, he had designed 21 buildings for the College.

"When we arrived as freshmen, there were only three permanent buildings—Johnson, Fowler, and Swan halls," Harold Wagner '24 once recalled. "There were narrow aprons of grass in front of the main buildings, together with macadam walkways. The rest of the Quadrangle was totally unimproved—bare adobe soil with little gulleys eroded by rainfall."

Long before he became Oxy's ninth president, student Arthur Coons '20 called for the beautification of campus in an editorial for *The Occidental*. Two decades later, President Remsen Bird brought that vision to life, working closely with famed landscape artist Beatrix Farrand to cultivate the natural beauty the College is known for today. Watching Farrand go about her duties—arriving on campus in a chauffeur-driven open touring car—"was a memorable experience all in itself," Addie (Grant) McMenamin '40 observed in 1990. "She was often dressed all in black from her large-brimmed hat to her full-length skirt. She would walk regally around the Quad, and then spend hours sitting on her camp stool, watching the flow of foot traffic while working on her plan for the campus."

Alumni Ave. April 1915

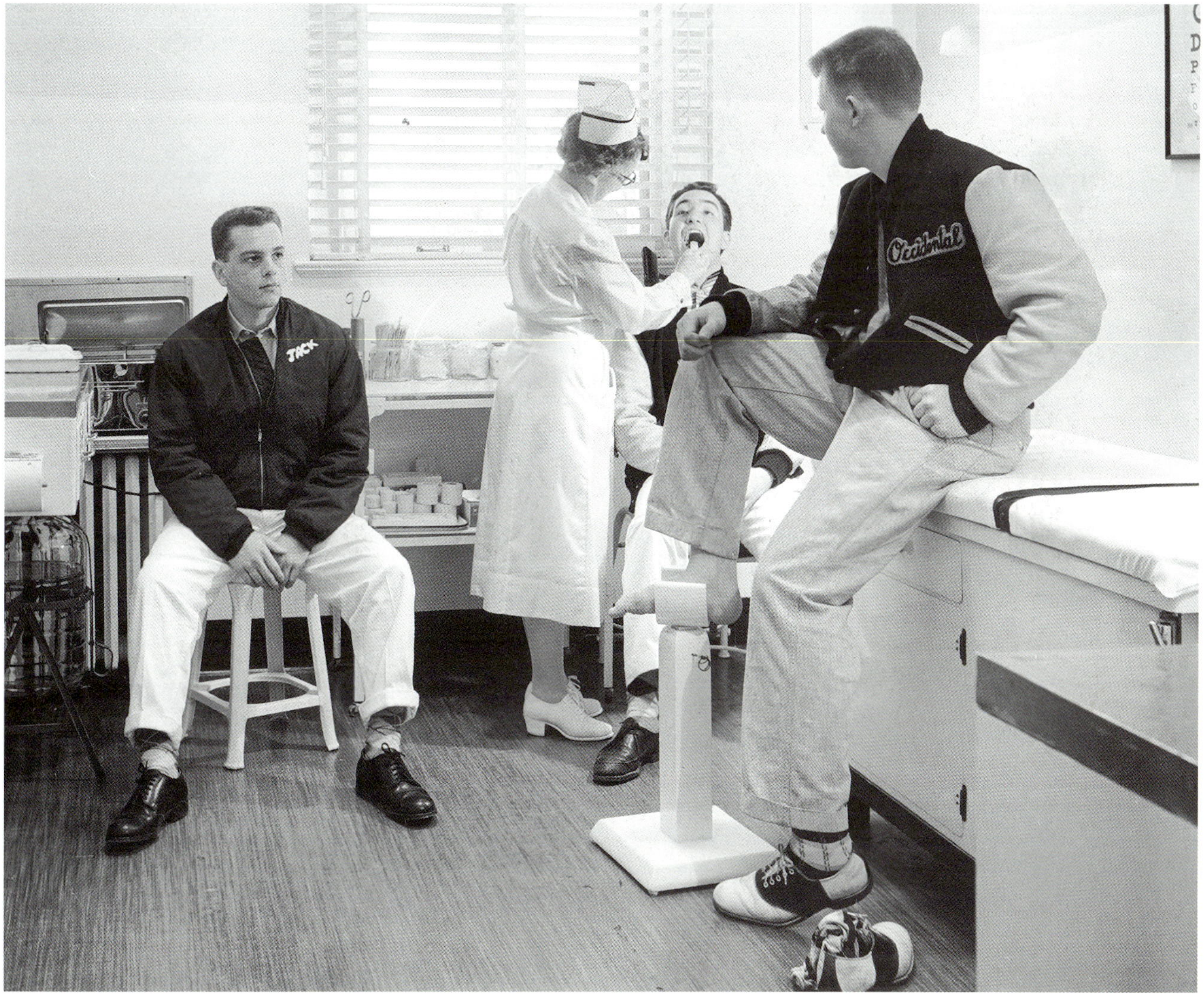

As Florence Brady '19 observed in 1970 in presenting the history of the Class of 1920 at Fifty Year Club Day, students of that earlier era had much in common with those who came of age during the Vietnam War. There were doves and hawks, then called pacifists and militarists; there was compulsory military service; there was a dress revolt on campus, with men taking to denims nationwide to combat the high cost of clothing; there was a strong feminist movement; there were active political clubs on campus, with a majority of Oxy students in favor of Woodrow Wilson. There were new social regulations on campus (a student committee was appointed to wait upon the president and urge that dancing be legalized). There was, ahem, a drug problem surrounding the "annual joy festival of nitrous oxide." Finally, there were those who failed to stand when "Occidental Fair" was sung, prompting others to bemoan "the collapse of tradition."

Tradition, as we'll see, is a very elastic and enduring word.

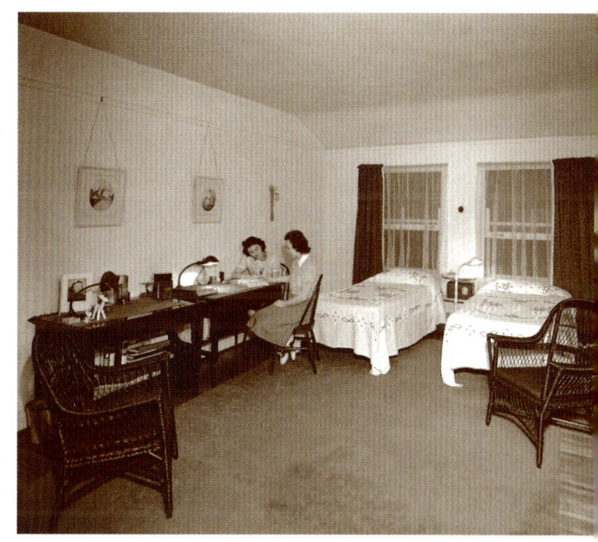

Fraternity and Justice for All

BELOW: From left, J.R. Kirkpatrick, A. Roy Thompson, Charles F. Bazata, A.W. Buell, Glen E. Huntsberger, and Lea Gorham—all members of the Class of 1904—celebrate the start of their junior year wearing the traditional plug-uglies in October 1902.

OPPOSITE: Members of the ASOC Council in 1930-31—all members of the Class of '31, unless noted—included (from left) Leonard Janofsky (president), Henry Shimanonshi (forensics representative), Zoe Rueger (secretary), Muriel Carlson (vice president), Alfred Ault (publications), Phil Ellswell '24 (graduate manager), adviser Florence Brady '19, Everett Moore (AMS president), David Roberts (rally representative), Mary Babcock (AWS president), and Richard Glover (athletics representative). "Our class was distinguished by the fact that during our senior year the faculty came up with the brilliant idea that seniors should take a comprehensive examination in their major," Janofsky recalled in 1981. "This was a first in the history of the College—and we were the unfortunate victims."

While the construction of Orr and Erdman halls in 1925 and 1927, respectively, transformed the Occidental experience for many, social organizations such as fraternities and sororities provided much of the entertainment of that era. "More and more informal campus and off-campus social affairs took place without benefit of chaperones," Si Johnson '32 recalled in 1982. "The dinner table at the fraternity house was always set for the number of members who lived in the house, but there were always several members who left the campus early on Fridays for the weekend, and so did not show up for dinner. So several members began to invite girls up to the house for Friday night dinner. It was a nice, inexpensive way to entertain."

The fraternity's hospitality caught the notice of Julia Pipal, head of residence and social activities, who requested a meeting with Johnson in her office at his earliest convenience. "As you might guess, the conversation had to do with having women guests at the fraternity house without proper chaperones," he continued. "She brushed aside my assurances that there was no hanky-panky involved and there was no harm done. She pointed out patiently that this was not the point, that there were many things that are not harmful but which we still refrain from doing because they are frowned upon by society. 'For instance,' she said, 'there is no harm in wearing a red tie with your tuxedo but you don't do it, nobody does it, because convention decrees that you wear a black tie with a tuxedo.'"

Before Johnson could think of "a good, snappy comeback," Pipal made it clear there was no more to be said. "As you might expect, we solved the problem the easy way. Instead of inviting chaperones, we simply stopped inviting the girls."

Other regulations of the era—such as a 10 p.m. curfew for women—"developed good work habits, the efficient use of time for one," Judge William Hogoboom '39 noted in 1989. "Much could be accomplished between the time the Cooler closed at 9 and lights out at 10 with attention to important detail. Having a good friend on the first floor who would open a window on occasion was good insurance."

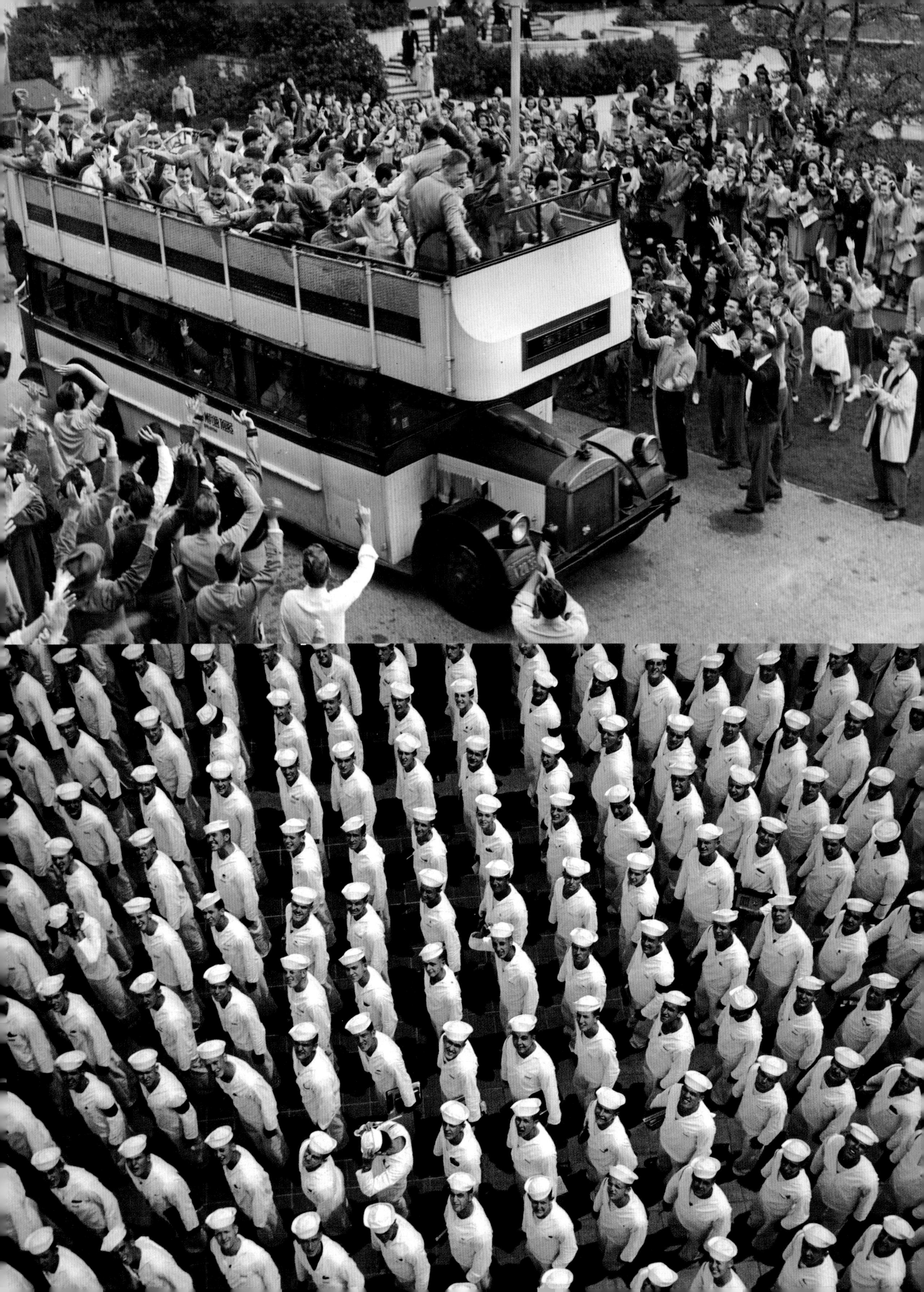

Life During Wartime

"One Saturday night in December 1941, some coeds left the campus to go to the show—the 'Dirty Dime' or the 'Filthy Fifteen,' depending upon which direction one went," Shirley (Wilson) Marlatt '44 recalled. "When the show was over and they walked back to campus, the full moon turned the Quad and steps of Johnson and Fowler to silver. They sat on the benches for quite a while to enjoy the beauty of the night."

On Sunday morning, President Remsen Bird interrupted the chapel service to announce that Pearl Harbor had been bombed. "The brilliant moonlight of the night before had led the Japanese Navy to sail unnoticed and make possible its sneak attack on Pearl Harbor," Marlatt said. "Right then, one world ended and another began."

ABOVE: *An anti-apartheid protest outside Freeman College Union in spring 1981. Five years later, students built a shantytown to encourage the College's divestment from companies operating in South Africa.*

BELOW: *ASOC president Don Cornwell '69 speaks to a group of student demonstrators in 1969.*

OPPOSITE: *Occidental students gathered outside the placement office to protest military recruitment on campus in April 1969.*

Occidental was a different place during World War II. Soon after Pearl Harbor, students signed up for ration books at a location off campus that allowed them to get meat, sugar, and coffee. Gas and tires were rationed, and off-campus events were no more. Huaraches replaced saddle shoes for ladies' footwear because they could be imported from Mexico without coupons.

With the help of President Bird and his staff, Oxy's Japanese students were transferred to colleges far from the West Coast, and "an emotional goodbye was enacted in the Union the night before they left," Marlatt said. As the war grinded on, air-raid warnings occurred "and we went into the basement of the dorms, waiting for we knew not what to happen."

In March 1946, six months after the war ended, the Phi Gamma Delta house had a wartime exhibition with artifacts from returning servicemen. As John Wright '49 tells the story, "There was one room for each theater of war, 300 trophies, swastika flags, samurai swords, guns, knives, bayonets, hand grenades, Teller mines, mortar shells, combat photos. With a huge Nazi swastika out in front, some of the neighbors thought the Fijis were starting World War III, and the police showed up before it was all explained."

Coca-Cola
Meadow Gold
HOMOGENIZED MILK
Work with ADLAI
STEVENSON
WIN with IKE
VOTE REPUBLICAN

Building on Tradition

From bonfires and barbecues to cheers and sagehen burials, Occidental's traditions are a motley crew. Some are fairly commonplace, while others are strangely, gloriously Oxy.

Bonfires sprang up around the time of the Pomona football rivalry, blazing strong from the teens through the 1950s. Oxy students joyously built a huge fire and burned a stand-in for Cecil, the Pomona mascot (a rubber chicken would suffice) the night before the game, then held a mock funeral service for it in Alumni Chapel after each victory. "We buried a lot of sagehens over the years," says Addie (Grant) McMenamin '40, who worked in the alumni office from 1959 to 1979.

"It was really pretty darn dangerous," says Andrew Rolle '43. "Those fires were maybe 20 feet tall! I think that some people occasionally would get burned." Today, under the careful supervision of the Los Angeles Fire Department, the bonfire has returned as a Homecoming tradition—provided the fall Santa Anas aren't blowing.

ABOVE: *ASOC presidents Lambert Baker '50, Ed Harper '51, Bill Evans '52, Allen "Red" Gresham '53, and Bruce Gilliland '54 line up for a photo in 1954.*

LEFT: *Freshman Bill Paden '61 (accompanied by stewardess Barbara MacIntire) prepares to depart from Burbank for Honolulu via Trans Continental Airlines, courtesy of the sophomore class in fall 1957. The bad news: It was a two-day trip. (That's hazing chairman Steve Beck '60 wishing him "Aloha.")*

OPPOSITE, TOP: *Built in 1928, the Tiger Cooler (shown here in 1952) has given generations of students a quick meal fix or a place to gather for chatter.*

OPPOSITE, BOTTOM: *Ike or Adlai? Students rally behind their favorite presidential candidate at a campus political rally on Oct. 9, 1952.*

Many of the guests at Melissa Lostaunau Palmer '88's wedding must have been at a loss for words. "I married a man whose family boasts Oxy grads on both sides," she explains. During the 1990 ceremony, "My husband's father and uncles serenaded me with 'Io Triumphe!'"

It's a cheer that 1907 graduate Frank Beal brought from his hometown in Albion, Mich., to Occidental in 1905. Soon thereafter, it was required learning for freshmen:

Io Triumphe! Io Triumphe!
Haben, swaben, rebecca le animor,
Whoop-te, whoop-te, sheller-de-vere-de,
Boom-de, ral-de, I-de, pa
Honeka, heneka, wack-a. wack-a
Hob, dob, bolde, bara, bolde, bara
Con, slomade, hob-dab—rah!
O! C! RAH!

BELOW: *Members of the Class of 1970 get their bearings during Orientation Week in 1966.*

OPPOSITE, TOP: *"Oxytwigs" Elliot Oppenheim '69, left, and Rex Weyler '70 perch among the limbs of a Prodocarpus elongatus, a longtime resident of the Quad, in an effort to save the pine from maintenance crew saws in March 1969.*

OPPOSITE, BOTTOM: *Freeman Union manager Clancy Morrison welcomes Gregory Peck (father of Jonathan Peck '66) to a campus event in 1964.*

"Everybody on campus was supposed to know it," Jim Cerveny '61 recalls. "Older students would stop you and ask you to repeat it. If you didn't know it, you had to do some crazy thing like push-ups. The thing was, it took time to memorize because it was just by word of mouth. They didn't give you a piece of paper so you could study it; you had to remember what they were saying. Now, when we're done giving awards and I get up in Thorne at the end of the year, I lead the chant. Everybody yells it and we walk away happy."

The honor spirit began in 1915 as a means of flushing out a few cheaters, but evolved into a way of life. Students felt free to leave their belongings strewn across the campus lawns without worrying about theft. "No tests were ever proctored," Ginny (Goss) Cushman '55 recalls. "We would leave our purses on the Quad when we came to go to lunch. We never locked our dorm rooms because we didn't have anything to steal. "

Eventually, the world crept in, and the honor spirit could not live under its weight. Less innocent times called for greater vigilance, and now dorm rooms stay locked.

ABOVE: *Local philosopher Walter Pennington was a frequent visitor to campus in the '60s, '70s, and '80s.*

RIGHT: *Seniors Bob Boress, Steve Rountree, Dick Andrews, and Bob Niemack—all members of the Class of '71—strike a pose for* La Encina.

OPPOSITE, TOP: *With his parents' seal of approval, this freshman moves into Stewart-Cleland Hall (or Stewie— "We Use Only 100% Fresh Ingredients") in 1978.*

OPPOSITE, BOTTOM: *What's good for the goose is good for the gander, as Anita Austin '72, Janeth Smith '72, and Debbie Sanderson check out the guys from a bench in the Quad in 1970.*

Pranks for Nothing!

While the 1960s brought protests to campus, of course, there was plenty of room for good old-fashioned pranking as well. There was the time that Tim Moore '63—a second-generation student who came from a construction background—moved a Caterpillar tractor from one part of campus to another over the weekend, much to the bafflement of the crew. (Dean of students Ben Culley quickly zeroed in on his primary suspect.)

In fact, not much seemed to escape the attentive eye of Culley. When Swan Hall was converted from a dorm into an office for professors, the College decided to relocate the central flagpole from the site in front of Swan to the present site in front of what is now the Coons Administrative Center. "The new flagpole was delivered in pieces and welded together on the ground next to the hole where it now resides," Walter Scott '64 recalls. "They finished the welding and left the pole lying on the ground ready to erect the next day. Well, the boys of Stewie carried the flagpole up the hill and placed it into the second-floor window of Stewart-Cleland, where it remained until the maid discovered it the next morning. Dr. Culley made it very clear that we would be paying for the pole to be removed from the dorm and returned to the site, plus the costs of the crew that came out to put it up and found it missing." With the know-how of the physics majors among the group, they returned the slightly bent pole to its original location and paid for its repair out of the dorm social fund.

And the Beat Goes On

While traditions have been an important part of many students' experience at Occidental, the school's culture is far from static. Today's students might be surprised to learn, for instance, that not so long ago, women had to wear dresses on campus during the week. "When I came to Oxy, women were on one side of the campus and men were on the hill," Brenda Hill '71 recalls. "From Friday noon until Sunday morning you could wear shorts and pants. Things changed very quickly. By my sophomore year, the dorms were coed."

Emeritus President Richard Gilman, who led the College through a particularly transformative stretch during the 1960s, believes that the College has aged well because of its ability to adapt: "The problem is not change in and of itself when it comes to administrative responsibility and leadership. It's the marriage of change and controlling the pace of change."

Cheers through the Years
OSWALD & COMPANY

In the century or so since Occidental adopted the colors orange and black for its athletes (and borrowed the tiger mascot from its inspiration to the east, Princeton), the College's cheerleaders have tried on many looks. So, too, has Oswald, who has evolved from a rally tiger suitable for travel (in a specially made packing case suitable for an 80-pound Bengal) to a flesh-and-blood student inside a famously cumbersome suit over the years.

Suzo McKellar '58 recalls her stint as Oswald with a mixture of humor and horror. "In my day, being asked to be the tiger was a big deal," she says. "You would run around on the football field, and no one knew who was inside. When you took it off, you were absolutely sweaty. No one told you that because you're not supposed to tell how bad it was inside the suit. I almost fainted."

TOP: Yell leaders Art Lewis '62, Terry Gilliam '62, and Bill Cook '61 give it the old college try in this 1960 photo.

ABOVE: Superfans Jesse Roberts '07, George Pechmann '06, and Cameron Brahmst '09 leave no doubt as to their school spirit during the Tigers' 57-36 Homecoming win over La Verne in November 2005, while Blair Bergsteinsson '10 (then a senior at Palos Verdes Peninsula High School) adds an exclamation mark to the proceedings.

RIGHT: Bill Hogoboom '39 and Bob Sheahan '39 wield their megaphones during a 1936 football contest.

ABOVE LEFT: *Cheerleader Pam Lee '77 and Oswald are all smiles after the Tigers' dramatic, come-from-behind 36-24 Homecoming victory over Pomona in 1974.*

ABOVE RIGHT: *Oswald joins participants from Oxy's Crossroads Africa program in 1958: (front row, l-r) John Paden '59, Jim Taylor '58, and Skip Day '59; (middle row) Aaron Segal '59, Dick Wright '58, Don Campbell '59, and Dave Stenger '59; (back row) Allana Crothers '59, Velma Montoya '59, and Ann Vine '59.*

LEFT: *An Oswald for a new century joins the Oxy cheerleaders and a young Tigers fan in 2005.*

RIGHT: *Participants in the inaugural Women of Oxy calendar included (standing, l-r) Sue Eidson '84, Cathy Isham '86, Val Coleman '85, Laura Speidel '86, Tammy Odom '83, Lisa Boisset '84, Valerie Hoebel '87; (sitting, l-r) Becky Hinton '86 and Lisa Coscino '85. The project grew out of a business plan written by Vy Rollins '84, Lynne Watson '83, and photographer Glenn Mar '84 for professor Derek Shearer's Urban Business class.*

BELOW: *An Alpha Tau Omega fraternity ritual was "Coming Out the Door," in which new pledges jumped off the Freeman College Union balcony into the arms of their brothers, as in this 1983 photo.*

OPPOSITE, TOP: *For the* Men of Oxy *calendar, Jason Oshima '83 poses inside the utility tunnel below the Union tower.*

OPPOSITE, BOTTOM: *Dean of students Brig Knauer, dean of faculty James England, and director of admission Jim Montoya did a send-up of* Flashdance *for a 1983 skit during Community Weekend—an annual excuse for fun and bonding between students and staff against the backdrop of the mountains.*

Speaking of marriage, the tradition that is often held up as an example is the one that is hardest to prove: the "Oxy Statistic." The way Tara Emrick '98 heard it as a freshman, 60 percent of Oxy students marry Oxy students. (The number varies from source to source, but it seems high regardless.)

The Occidental Weekly looked into the matter in April 2007, interviewing a number of couples who fit the profile, from Allen Gresham '53 and Clara (Thompson) Gresham '53 (who were married by an Oxy chaplain in 1954) to Doug Carlsen '72 and Vicki (Young) Carlsen '72 (who traded vows in December 2003—18 months after meeting at their 30th reunion) to Jason Reade '98 and Eddie Jauregui '01 (who held their commitment ceremony on March 17, 2007, on campus).

As for Emrick, she held up her end of the bargain, tying the knot with Bryan Kono '99 on Dec. 17, 2000. "One moment you are stressed about a final, thinking about that night's party, and thinking about your summer vacation, and the next you meet your future husband," she observed in 2001. "Marrying your soulmate is very lucky, but having your soulmate be a fellow Oxy student is the most amazing blessing of all."

One undisputed truth is the abiding sense of camaraderie that ties generations of Occidental graduates. From Fifty Year Club Weekend, a reunion tradition dating to 1954, to newer programs such as the CASE award-winning Oxy Eclectic, a recurring showcase for young alumni musicians, alumni events draw more than 5,000 participants each year. (Even the annual Volunteer Leadership Conference, established in 2001, attracts more than 125 participants eager to help out the College in fund- and friend-raising programs alike.) "One of the fringe benefits of a small school is that I can come to an event 50 years out and always find someone I know," says Ann Moyes '53. "When you go to a big school, you could go to 100 events and never see anyone."

And that doesn't take into account the informal alumni gatherings that reunite old friends in places far and near. Whether it's a Gamma pledge reunion at Judy Harris '68's vacation home in Truckee or a Sigma Alpha Epsilon ski weekend spearheaded by Tim Moore '63 and company, or the quarterly get-togethers of the "Girls of Oxy '53," the College connection persists despite time and location.

Perhaps the best reunions of all are those chance encounters—at a taco truck in Eagle Rock, at a Dodgers game in the late September heat, stuck on the freeway and spying an Oxy license plate, or even halfway around the world where "Io Triumphe!" is lost in translation. Everyone's a student once again.

ABOVE: *Shoshone Johnson '09 and a fellow student hit the books.*

OPPOSITE, TOP: *The wettest California winter in more than a century took its toll on Oxy, toppling trees, flooding the Quad, and closing down campus for two power-hungry days in February 2005.*

OPPOSITE, BOTTOM: *Thirty-foot flames lick the night sky as hundreds of spectators watch the traditional Homecoming bonfire in 2005—a tradition believed to date back to Occidental's first football game with Pomona in 1895.*

FANGs for the Memory
AND NOW FOR SOMETHING COMPLETELY

ABOVE: *Editor Paul Bertness '50 and art editor Tom Trotter '50 hard at work in the Fang office: "It remains vivid after 60 years," Trotter says.*

BELOW: *Tom Trotter's cover to Fang's debut issue in 1946, left, and a typically Gilliamesque cover to Fang from 1961.*

OPPOSITE: *An assortment of Fang covers from 1948, 1957, and 1961.*

By his own typewritten admission—mimeographed and inserted into his debut issue—editor-in-chief Urban G. Whitaker Jr. '46 was "quaking in his boots pending *Fang*'s campus reception in December 1946. First, it must sell and sell well or it will be the last *Fang* ever published. Second, it must meet some kind of student approval if it is to be continued. Third, there are many things wrong with this infant"—including due recognition of his writers and giving credit (and a lifetime subscription) to Betsy Keyes '48, who dreamed up the publication's name.

Of the student journals published in the 20th century—among them *Sabertooth* (a magazine of poems, prose, cartoons, and jokes, published from 1920 to 1943), *Tawney Cat* (a humor magazine, published from 1927 to 1930), and *Occidental Review* (a literary journal which first appeared in the 1960s)—none left a more lasting impression than *Fang*.

DIFFERENT

While Tom Trotter '50's Tigers graced its covers from the outset, Whitaker (a political science major who graduated after putting the first issue to bed, he went on to teach international relations as a professor at San Francisco State University) envisioned *Fang* not as a humor journal, but as a "campus digest"—a hybrid of *Time* and *The New Yorker*. In the first issue, for instance, there were items on new President Arthur G. Coons '20, the ASOC budget, athletics, and a handful of cartoons; by the next issue, there was a page of jokes.

In short order, *Fang* evolved into the familiar mix of opinion pieces, satire, reviews, sketches, and miscellany that defined much of its 22-year run. One oasis of visual relief—and a constant over its many iterations dating back to 1948—was the *Fang* Queen, a page or more of pinup shots devoted to a comely Oxy coed (beginning with Frances Matthes '48).

Fang's most famous alumnus is Terry Gilliam '62, who took the reins of the magazine as a junior and trained his satiric eye toward making *Fang* the Oxy equivalent of *Mad*—he even mailed copies to founding editor Harvey Kurtzman—turning out six issues a semester at his anarchic peak. "Basically, we turned what was originally a high-class art and poetry magazine into a cheap comic," Gilliam said in a 1995 interview with Paul Wardle published in *The Comics Journal*. "It was good fun. We were cartooning, writing, editing, everything."

Since *Fang* breathed its last in spring 1968, several attempts have been made to revive the publication by later generations of students. None have lasted, and maybe *Fang*'s time had come and gone. Most 22-year-olds move on after college—but some of them, thankfully, never grow up.

Praise Uproarious

Trevor Norton '91's earliest memory of the Occidental Summer Theater festival is a moment he never saw. "I wanted so badly to see the surrey ('With the Fringe on Top') at the end of *Oklahoma!* that I begged for my family to wake me up," he recalls (he slept through it every time). In the summer of 1979, at the ripe old age of 11, he earned $300 working for the festival as a lighting assistant—and he returned every summer for the next 20 years.

ABOVE: *Actors Chris Shelton '68 M'69 and Patricia Mitchell '69 make eyes in the 1967 Summer Theater production of Jean Anouilh's Ring Around the Moon.*

LEFT: *Designed by Myron Hunt to serve the College and the community, Hillside Theater hosted its inaugural production, Euripides's Iphigenia in Aulis, in 1925.*

The format of the festival—created by professor of theater arts and rhetoric Omar Paxson '48 at the suggestion of dean of the faculty Glenn Dumke '38—was simple: five plays in repertory, with a heavy rotation of staples from Shakespeare, Gilbert and Sullivan, and Bernard Shaw ("so we wouldn't have to pay royalties," says Paxson). Rehearsals ran for four to five weeks every weeknight from 7 p.m. to midnight, with an epic rehearsal each Saturday. Though the directors and other professionals were paid a small stipend, the bulk of the troupe came from Oxy's student body. "Omar always used to say, 'Everybody makes the popcorn!' And that's what made the Summer Theater experience so extraordinary," says Lucy Lee '78. "You would play a lead on Thursday, be in a Gilbert and Sullivan chorus on Friday, and tear tickets at the door on Saturday."

The first season unfolded on a makeshift stage in front of Thorne Hall. It was a great success, netting almost $1,000—enough to finance the project for another summer. In the space of a few years, the program grew so popular that it was moved to its permanent quarters at the Hillside Theater, which was upgraded to include dressing rooms, a ticket booth, and new restrooms. Future Tony Award-winning actress Swoosie Kurtz worked for the festival her first summer out of high school; another eventual Tony winner, Joanna Gleason '72, was directed by Paxson's longtime friend, actor and Beverly Hills High School drama teacher John Ingle '50, who worked for the festival for 10 years en route to TV's "General Hospital."

While the curtain came down on the Summer Theater Festival at the turn of the century, its spirit lives on not only in Occidental College Children's Theater—where Rodgers and Hammerstein meets Rocky and Bullwinkle each summer under the direction of Jamie Angell—but also in the annual New Play Festival, in which short student-written plays (including the occasional contribution by non-theater majors) are staged by a mix of students and professionals each spring with the guiding hand of adjunct theater instructor Laural Meade '88. "Omar Paxson used to say, 'Theater problems are happy problems,'" recalls Meade. "Sounds corny, but it's true. Our work as theater artists—although incredibly complicated, difficult, and multifaceted—has a lightheartedness to it."

Everybody still makes the popcorn at Occidental.

SPOTLIGHT

Alan Freeman '66 M'67
PROFESSOR OF THEATER

Patricia Mitchell '69 (Major Barbara), John Ingle '50 (father Andrew Underschaft), and Freeman (Adolphus Cusins) in a publicity shot for George Bernard Shaw's Major Barbara *(1966), directed by Omar Paxson '48. "Cusins wears the drum in Act 2 in a wonderful duet scene with his soon-to-be father-in-law," Freeman explains. "At the end of an exuberant speech where Cusins trumpets his adoration for Barbara, he beats the drum as an acoustic exclamation point. I always thought it should get a laugh, or chuckle, or some kind of vocal acknowledgment from the audience. Instead, it got a lot of silence." Years later, when Freeman directed the play in Keck Theater, "I tried once again to get a laugh in coaching our new Cusins (Ryan Rogers '94) to beat it just so ... More silence." He eventually saw the 1941 film, with Rex Harrison in the role of Cusins, and "He beat the drum, too, just as it calls for in the script. He didn't get a laugh, either."*

Alan Freeman '66 M'67's connection with Oxy runs deep; not only were his parents both alumni, but his grandfather served as a trustee for four decades and as longtime board chair. As a typically rebellious teenager, though, Freeman was unimpressed by tradition. "I had been to the College a couple of times," he recalls, "but I had no sense of the campus at all. While I was still in high school, I was driving down the Pasadena Freeway and saw the Occidental College sign. I drove over to campus and just fell in love with it."

And so it came about that Freeman matriculated in fall 1962. During his undergraduate years at Oxy, he was consumed by his work for the theater department and his passion for the Glee Club. At the time, he was a recent convert to the arts; he had an affinity for the hard sciences in high school until he auditioned for *Stalag 17*, loved it, and decided to change paths.

After he earned his M.A., Freeman joined the world of professional theater in Los Angeles and then San Francisco, where he worked for the Western Opera Theater (the touring arm of the San Francisco Opera). It wasn't long before Oxy drew him back in; at the urging of his mentor, Omar Paxson '48, Freeman returned to teach in 1969.

"Opportunity brought me back, along with the passion to do more than I was able to do while I was away," he says. "I've known since how easy it is in an academic environment for a practicing artist to get stale. I decided that I wouldn't let myself do that. I reevaluated every year to decide whether or not to do another year. I did that with a great deal of seriousness for 10 years. I found that, for me, Oxy was a place that I would continue to grow for a long time."

That decision long behind him, Freeman has indeed had time to flourish. He has cultivated new interests, including filmmaking, which he studied as a fellow at the American Film Institute during a year-long sabbatical. As it turned out, Freeman wasn't really so different from his forefathers; no longer a willful 18-year-old, he has no need to hide his dedication to the school that has served as his family's second home for generations.

ABOVE: Alan Freeman's grandparents, the Rev. Robert Freeman and the former Margery Fulton, in an undated photo. The couple was married in 1909.

LEFT: A Freeman family portrait in Keck Theater, taken for Occidental Magazine in fall 2001: clockwise from lower right, wife Kathie (Cole) Freeman '65 M'72, Alan Freeman '66 M'67, sister Zoe (Freeman) Rowe '56, son Christopher Freeman '91, daughter Megan Freeman '89, and granddaughter Fiona Freeman-Grundei, then 3.

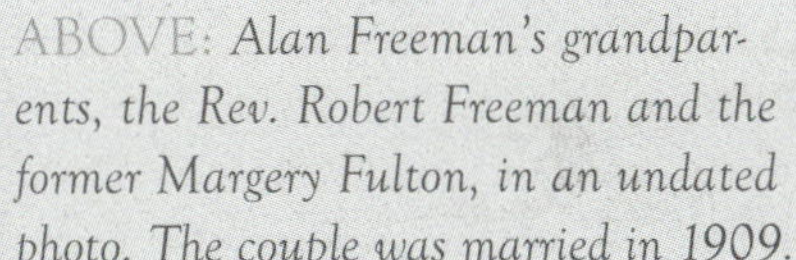

Encouraging the Arts

Occidental has long recognized that the fine arts are an integral component of a first-rate liberal arts education.

In its infancy, the College dedicated its class time to a bare-bones classical curriculum. The first published catalog in 1888 noted that instruction in music (vocal and instrumental), painting, and drawing was available for an additional $4 per month, but course offerings wouldn't become the norm until a department of fine arts was formed in 1927. Informal interest in the creative arts was strong from the very beginning, in part because of the efforts of William Dennis Ward, a beloved classics professor who is best remembered for composing "Occidental Fair" (with music by his daughter, Ethel Ward Johnson). He almost single-handedly brought Greek drama to the campus.

The '20s ushered in a time of profound growth, particularly in the fine arts, when President Remsen Bird (who in retirement would serve on the board of trustees of the Foundation for Environmental Design alongside photographer and longtime friend Ansel Adams) overhauled the curriculum after World War I. In 1923, a speech department was founded to formalize the study of debate and drama. A full music department was established three years later. Its director, Walter E. Hartley, founded Occidental's first full orchestra in 1927.

Even college professors sometimes have to moonlight to pay the bills, though. Charles Frederick Lindsley, who taught speech in the 1930s, supplemented his faculty salary by reading radio commercials, which could be a distraction. "Kurt Baer staged a performance of *Everyman* in the Greek Theater during our junior year," John Espey '35 recalled in 1985. "The entire audience rippled with a stir hard to characterize—surely it was not one of ribaldry—when the voice of God boomed out over the loudspeakers in the unmistakable and measured tones of White King Soap. For that night, cleanliness *was* godliness."

OPPOSITE: Professor Charles Frederick Lindsley instructs Bob Finch '47 and Phyllis Nisbit King '45 in the use of the microphone, which was described in a 1945 Oxy press release as "one of many pieces of modern equipment that Dr. Lindsley and his fellow members of the speech department use in their work."

BELOW: Professor William Dennis Ward (shown here in 1914) taught Latin and classics and Greek at the College for many years and was known affectionately as the "Grand Old Man of Occidental."

The arts at Occidental continued to evolve during the Great Depression, though more slowly. The College received a Carnegie grant in 1934 that helped fund the music department's library of scores and recordings. Office space in Thorne Hall was allocated to speech and drama faculty in 1938.

Art professors like J. Donald Young, Constance Perkins, and Robert Hansen had to wait a bit longer for their department to bloom. In 1955, they celebrated the completion of a new art building. When Young retired in 1962, the department began drawing more interest from students who were excited by contemporary artists like Andy Warhol. Student art, which was shown regularly in Thorne Hall and in the Art Barn, grew more sophisticated, and other instructors in the arts made lasting impressions as well. In his all-too-brief career at Occidental (1965-1969), Bill Moritz's "impromptu, occasionally all-night film festivals in Mosher were legendary, and the cinema classes that he and Marsha Kinder ran were probably the finest in the country at that time," Bill Hawkins '69 wrote following Moritz's death (at age 62) in 2004.

SPOTLIGHT

George Baker '58
PROFESSOR OF ART

George Baker '58 was an internationally acclaimed sculptor who was discovered by the same curator who introduced the painter Francis Bacon to Los Angeles. The Corsicana, Texas, native's work has appeared in top museums all over the world, including the Museum of Modern Art and the Whitney Museum of American Art in New York. His best-known works—massive wind sculptures and kinetic fountains—aptly symbolize his influence in the art world.

But to generations of Oxy alumni, Baker is best remembered for his role as a teacher. Like many of his colleagues in the visual and performing arts, he chose to practice his craft in a tight-knit liberal arts environment.

After four years of teaching at USC, where he completed his MFA in 1960, he returned to Occidental as a professor of sculpture in 1964. There, he created some of his most significant works with the help of his students, who knew him not only as a great artist, but also as a dedicated mentor.

"George Baker gave me the only F in my college career," recalls professor Alan Freeman '66 M'67, whose long hours in the theater as an undergraduate made him one of the sculptor's most lackluster students. "As a senior, I took sculpture, thinking that it would be really fun. I was so overcommitted and undermanaged that I never could go to the class. It never dawned on me to drop it because I was in denial.

"The poor guy had to give me an F. He tracked me down. He tried for days and days to find me, to find some way to get me to come in. He would send me notes and try to call. I was too ashamed and embarrassed. When I came back as a faculty member, we could laugh about it. He was still pained, though; I had to assure him that it was not his fault."

Recent generations of Oxy students who never knew him in his lifetime are intimately familiar with one of his signature works—*Water Forms II*, the kinetic fountain that graces Alumni Drive. Measuring 26 feet long, 15 feet wide, and 12 feet high, it was created as a memorial to Lucille Gilman, President Richard Gilman's late wife, in 1979. A second installation, *Arc Forms, Three Axis* (also known as *Wind Forms*)—completed prior to Baker's death in 1997—is located near Samuelson Pavilion and was a gift to the College by friends of the artist "in loving memory and in recognition of a life devoted to the ideals of art and to the students of Occidental."

ABOVE: *The Art Barn was home to sculpture classes taught by Baker prior to 1994.*

BELOW: *Baker in his studio in an undated photo.*

OPPOSITE: Wind Forms (*1997, top*) *was installed on campus following Baker's death, while* Water Forms II (*1979, bottom*)*, a kinetic fountain designed by Baker in memory of Lucille Gilman, gained additional visibility as a Vulcan hot spot in the 1984 film* Star Trek III: The Search for Spock.

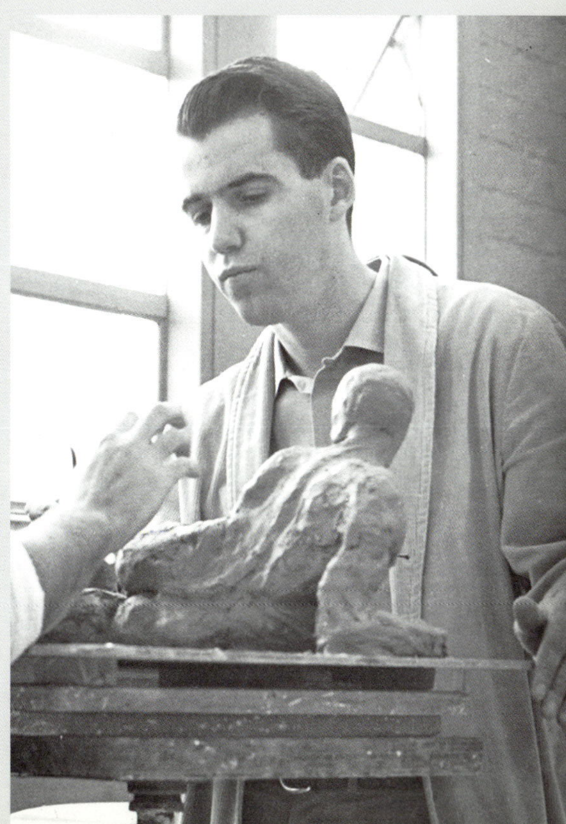

RIGHT: *Against the background
of a larger canvas that will become
the finished piece, Meilani Bowman-
Kamaha'o '10 works on a study for
professor Linda Stark's Intermediate
Painting class in fall 2007.*

BELOW: *Emily Birnbaum '06, Emily
Harkins '08, and Megan Becker '08
perform in a workshop production of*
The Beauty Myth *by Lisa Szolovit
'06, part of the New Play Festival
staged by the Theater Department
in February 2006.*

Engaging the Arts

The arts at Occidental have never been limited to the classroom or the studio; throughout the College's history, Oxy faculty have worked to create opportunities that reward more than class participation. Some of the College's most illustrious alumni rounded out their educations through informal involvement in the arts, like the young Arthur Coons '20. Many years before he served as president, Coons spent long hours with the theater department, beginning with his first semester, when he landed a role in *The Dearest Bride.*

Today, Occidental's approach to the arts is participatory, providing students with formal and informal opportunities to explore their talents and interests. Oxy trains artists, but it also teaches students from across disciplines to use the arts as a critical lens through which to see the world.

Theater professor Alan Freeman '66 M'67 firmly believes that creating art is an instructive exercise for everyone. "I treat everybody in my acting classes as if they intend to be professional actors, knowing full well that not all of them do," he explains. "Why would I want to teach any other way? It would be cheating them. I teach the discipline at the level of the most engaged, rather than teaching it as arts appreciation. Art does not need to be appreciated; it needs to be done. Biology appreciation? Psychology appreciation? The idea is ridiculous."

ABOVE: *From 1969 until his retirement in 2001, professor of music Richard Grayson mixed and matched all manner of musical forms—imagine "Over the Rainbow" in the style of Brahms, or Beethoven's "Moonlight Sonata" as an Irish gig—for his always entertaining improvisational concerts in Thorne Hall.*

BELOW: *Jennifer Reid '08, an arts history and the visual arts and psychology major from Pasadena, plies her skills for a portrait in clay.*

OPPOSITE: *Jacinda Wortman '06, Alice Hammond '08, and Shannon Sullivan '08 (top) rehearse alongside their fellow performers for Oxy's Dance Production in 2006. The popular annual event, which features the work of student dancers and choreographers (such as this Hawaiian-themed number from 2005, bottom), began as an outgrowth of the Occidental Dance Group, founded in the early 1940s by Patricia (McGrath) White '43. "I was just carrying on what I had been doing professionally," says White, who had danced for the Lester Horton Dance Group ("the Martha Graham of the West Coast").*

Part of what makes Oxy's liberal arts tradition special is that the curriculum is set up to create the kinds of learning opportunities that can only occur when students are pushed outside of their comfort zones. Freeman particularly treasures contributions from students who are not theater majors. "It's so exciting to be teaching a play or a scene and have somebody say, 'We were talking about that in psychology class,'" he notes. "It's thrilling that suddenly this becomes a palpable object lesson for what students are learning in another class. It happens all the time."

"There is this notion that art is something that comes from the divine; you either have it or you don't," Freeman says. "I love debunking that. It's one of the worst fallacies our culture has promoted. Everyone can be an artist who is competent to a point of self-fulfillment. The arts are a point of view, a way of looking at life around you and reshaping it into something that suggests a greater whole than what is there. Practicing that is an empowering discipline."

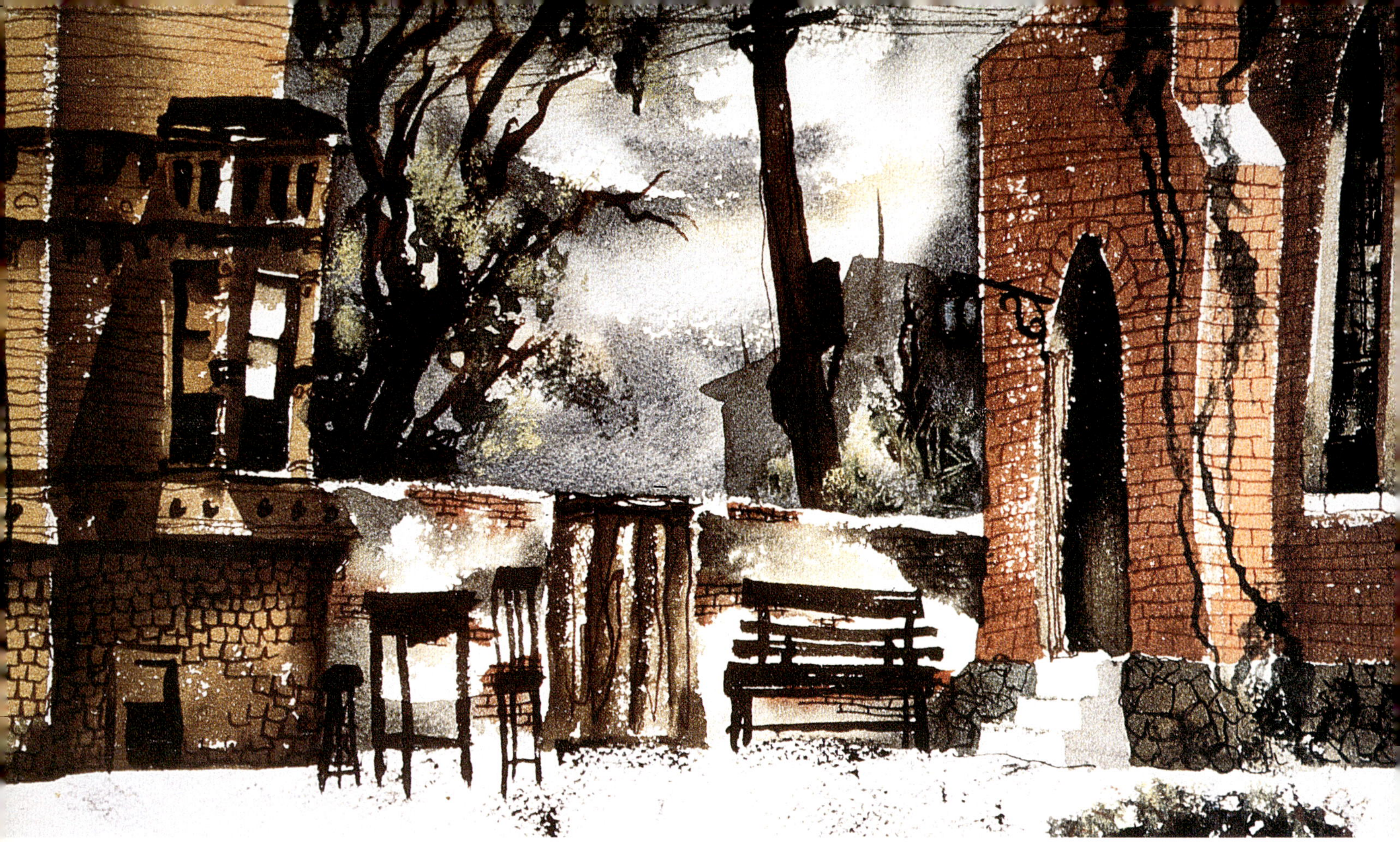

ABOVE: *Ming Cho Lee '53's watercolor sketch for* The Silver Whistle *(1952), produced by the Occidental Players (opposite page)—his very first theatrical credit as a designer. (He also had a small part as an undertaker.) The 2003 National Medal of Arts honoree and dean of American set designers, below, changed the face of theater with his groundbreaking work for the New York Shakespeare Festival.*

Ambassadors of Excellence

Occidental nurtures the arts in its classrooms and after hours, but ultimately their starring role is off campus. Generations of able artists have successfully made the transition from the studios and stages of the College to those in the wider world.

More than a few alumni have gone on to international acclaim in his or her chosen field. Pianists Martha Baird Rockefeller '16 and John Browning '55 were hailed among the world's top interpreters of Chopin and Ravel, respectively. Oscar-winning documentary filmmaker Marcel Ophuls '50 (*Hotel Terminus: The Life and Times of Klaus Barbie*) majored in philosophy and credits professor Cyril Gloyn '27 as a mentor. (His empiricism "was a way of looking at reality that began to suit me very well," Ophuls said in 2005.) Even Jason Sellards '00—better known to pop music fans as Scissor Sisters front man Jake Shears—did the sound design for a 1996 Theater Department production of *A Murder of Crows* during his sole year at Oxy: "It definitely gave me a lot of confidence to make music," he told *Occidental Magazine* in 2005.

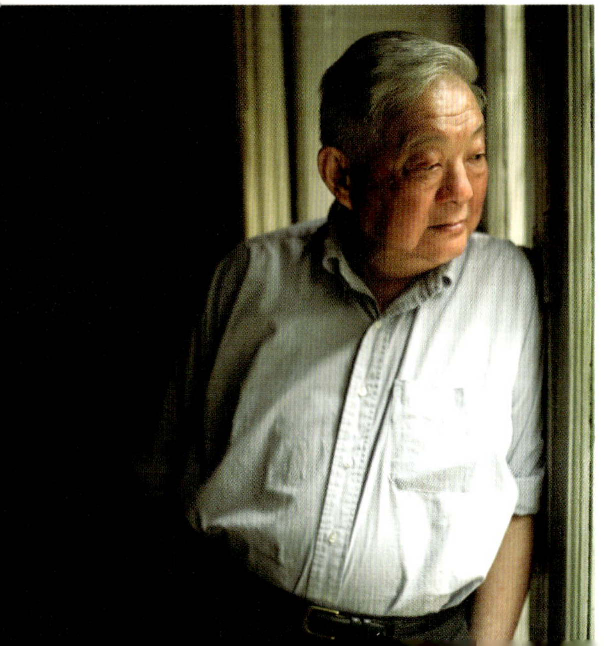

More frequently, Oxy alumni use their fine arts training to build successful careers that are high profile in professional circles, if not the public eye. Ming Cho Lee '53—Yale professor, legendary set designer, and winner of the National Medal of the Arts—got his first theatrical credit as a designer for a Paxson production of *The Silver Whistle*. Classmate George Stevens Jr. founded the American Film Institute in 1967 and created the Kennedy Center Honors a decade later. And Cheri (Eichen) Steinkellner '77 won a pair of Emmys as an executive producer of "Cheers," and has since plied her talents on the award-winning animated series "Teacher's Pet" as well as working in the musical theater.

Welz Kauffman '83 studied music at Oxy long before he became CEO of the Ravinia Festival in Chicago. Erik Nash '84, meanwhile, designed his own major (visual communications) before he created the special effects that would earn him an Oscar nomination for *I, Robot* in 2005. "I think it made me better prepared for the different challenges along the way," he says. "It's funny how art history will rear its head now and then as I will struggle to remember a certain painter. I don't know if that's the kind of thing they teach in film school."

ABOVE: *"Teacher's Pet" co-creator Cheri Steinkellner '77 and her cast, as depicted by collaborator Gary Baseman.*

BELOW: *Tim Stanford '75 developed his love for the stage watching his brother in a Summer Theater production; later, he became artistic director of New York Playwrights Horizon, a theater that promotes the work of new American writers, composers, and lyricists (including the 2007 Tony-winning Grey Gardens).*

Still, Oxy's best-traveled ambassadors of artistic excellence can be found right on campus. The Occidental Glee Clubs gained international acclaim under choral conductor Howard Swan, who came to the College in 1934. By mid-century, choral music great Robert Shaw opined that Occidental's singers were "one of the finest collegiate choral ensembles in America." To cite just one example, in 1961 the Glee Clubs sang at the invitation of conductor Bruno Walter in an all-Brahms recording session for Columbia Records. Though he left Occidental in 1971 at the then-mandatory retirement age of 65 and died in 1995, Swan left an indelible mark on the College and generations of students (a fact reinforced at a centennial celebration of the choruses in 2006).

Though the groups' membership ebbed and flowed under Swan's successors, Hal Gibbons (1971-1977) and Thomas Somerville (1977-1997), they returned to prominence under the baton of Jeffrey Bernstein (1997-2008), who became only the sixth full-time choral director in Oxy history. (Occidental appealed to the then-30-year-old director of choral activities at Harvard for two reasons: the Glee Clubs' longevity and the availability of quality venues—Thorne Hall and Herrick Chapel—in which to sing.)

"For something like this to survive 100 years, there has to be some deep, valuable experience that inspires generations of students," Bernstein observed in 2006. "Almost all of the students in the Glee Clubs say it's an essential part of their Oxy experience, and frequently the most formative one."

Robert Bolyard '06 decided to enroll at Occidental after attending one of the Glee Clubs' concerts while he was still in high school. "They did Messiah, and it exceeded my expectations a great deal," he says. Bolyard desired a liberal arts education that would promote a more well-rounded curriculum and more deeply impact his skills and musical aspirations. He became a conducting student under Bernstein, a role that served him in good stead when he enrolled in Yale's choral conducting program after graduation. "There's no big ego pushing us," Bolyard says of his Glee Clubs experience. "It's very much a community of friends that makes good music together."

OPPOSITE, TOP: The Glee Club in 1984, under the direction of Thomas Somerville. "Coming in when I did was a real treat," says Somerville, who took the group to Europe twice in the 1980s as well as the former Soviet Union. Another staple of the Somerville era was the annual madrigal dinner, complete with period costumes, flaming pudding, and holiday music.

ABOVE AND OPPOSITE, BOTTOM: "People are in this for the intrinsic rewards of making beautiful music together with only their bodies as an instrument," says Somerville's successor as choral director, Jeffrey Bernstein (with the Glee Clubs in 2000). "It's a powerful, transcendent experience."

SPOTLIGHT

Howard Swan
CHORAL DIRECTOR

It should not come as a surprise that Howard Swan, who directed Occidental's Glee Clubs for almost four decades, has had a lasting impact on the College. Thirty-seven years of service is a long time, and then there's the fact that he was so good at his job that he was known and admired internationally. But those too young to remember him might be surprised by the near-mythical status accorded him by his former students.

Swan led the Glee Clubs through what many consider the groups' golden years, from 1934 to 1971. An interesting figure on campus, he was tall, lean, and severe, though a paralyzed vocal chord that transformed his baritone into a falsetto perhaps softened that last trait. He was brilliant, but also dedicated, arriving at his office most mornings by 6:30.

Ginny Cushman '55, who describes her Glee Club experience as "its own magical world," remembers being impressed by Swan's level of involvement with students who had long since graduated. "He never forgot a person," she says. "We would come back for alumni rehearsals and he would say, 'OK, Ginny, the altos are sitting there and I think you ought to sit next to...'"

Indeed, there must have been something magical about a person who convinced students to spend 4 1/2 hours rehearsing each week for just one credit per semester. He was exceptionally skilled and remarkably compelling, and it is that combination that perpetuates the Howard Swan legend. His legacy is not just the greatness he bestowed upon the College, but also the lives he continues to touch beyond the grave.

"Each generation of Occidental music students felt Dr. Swan belonged to them," says Gail (Nelson) Mickelson '43. "He made music a living thing. He taught us things we will never forget. And if there really is a heaven, and somehow we get there, the first thing we will see is Howard Swan directing the celestial choir."

ABOVE: *Got to rest those vocal chords: This Glee Club member catches a few winks en route to parts unknown during the groups' summer 1968 tour.*

LEFT: *Howard Swan and the Occidental Glee Clubs in January 1964. When he came to the College 30 years earlier at the invitation of athletic manager Ted Broadhead, his salary was $40 a month.*

OPPOSITE, TOP: *Howard Swan prepares to conduct a class that includes Bryce LaMatte '57, Bob Billings '56, Viola Fuehr '57, Kay Hickman '58, and Debbie Bepew '56.*

OPPOSITE, BOTTOM: *Carol Bostick '54 and Joel Davis '54 review a song under the watchful eye of Swan.*

ABOVE: Homecoming and Family Weekend visitors to Oxy enjoy a performance by the Children's Theater in 2007. Each summer director Jamie Angell adapts two traditional folk tales while also spinning an original yarn such as The Boy Who Cried Wolfman *(2004) or* Goldilocks and the Three Tenors *(2003).*

OPPOSITE: Angell and the 2004 Children's Theater troupe, including Angell's wife, Ursula (wearing orange), as well as Devon Carson '06 (blue), William Kaminski '05 (yellow), Betsy Hume '05 (green), Jennifer George '04 (purple), and Alex Trumbo '05 (red).

Occidental College Children's Theater has helped strengthen the connection between Oxy and the community by performing folk tales with a twist each summer since 1995. Artistic director Jamie Angell, who has worked on many merchandising tie-ins to childhood friend Matt Groening's masterwork, *The Simpsons*—from calendars and comic books to trading cards and the ever-popular *Bart Simpson's Guide to Life*—develops original plays performed by a six-member troupe that are colorful enough to entertain small children, clever enough to appeal to their parents, and creative enough to generate raves from area critics.

"Being in a rehearsal room with these actors, regardless of their experience, it's fun," Angell observed in 2004. "You're solving problems with a group of people who are interested in doing the same thing. Whether it's theater or biology or anything else, that's the most rewarding thing: You're working with people toward a common goal."

While individual programs and faculty members inevitably change over time, the power of the arts to inform or transform the lives of Oxy students is a tradition that will never fade. "I sometimes find that seeing a student production of *As You Like It* is much more important than seeing *The Producers*," says Ming Cho Lee. "In *As You Like It*, Shakespeare is exploring different facets of life, of falling in love, that is fantastic and funny and you come away and your perception of life has changed a little bit. That is what theater should do."

SPOTLIGHT

Lights! Cameras! Oxy!
THE COLLEGE AT THE CINEPLEX

From *The Cup of Fury* (based on a 1919 espionage potboiler by Rupert Hughes) to *Made of Honor* (a 2008 gender-switch knock-off of *My Best Friend's Wedding*), Occidental has long attracted Tinseltown—from the A-list to the D-list. Cinematically speaking, there have been more lows than highs (ask anyone who's endured a screening of 1999's *Boys and Girls*, in which Freddie Prinze Jr.'s Gopher-costumed mascot loses his head, which is crushed underneath the car belonging to Claire Forlani's homecoming queen). But for pure Oxy cinematic bliss buried in a mountain of low-budget cheese, it's futile to resist the charms of the roller-disco tour of campus—down the Quad, onto Patterson Field, and into the classroom in the 2 ½-minute opening sequence of 1980's *Midnight Madness*. Add it to your queue.

Horse Feathers, 1932

Yes Sir, That's My Baby, 1949

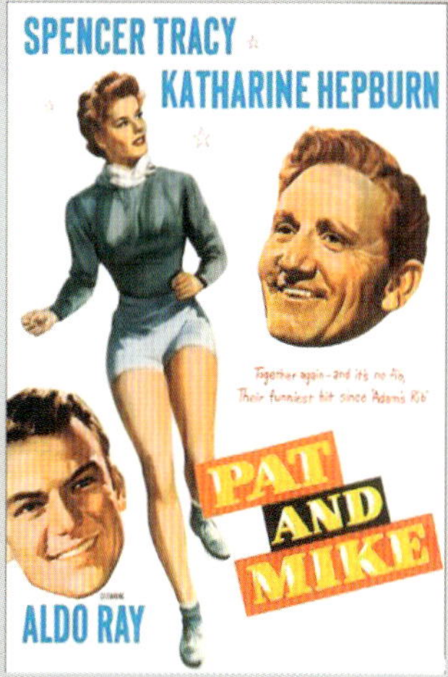

Pat and Mike, 1952

Tall Story, 1960

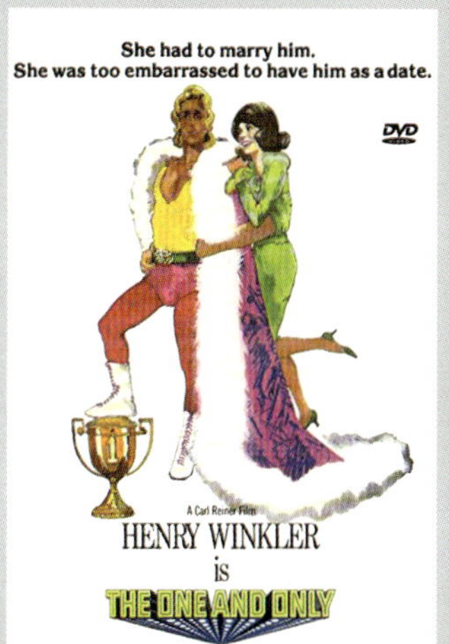

The One and Only, 1978

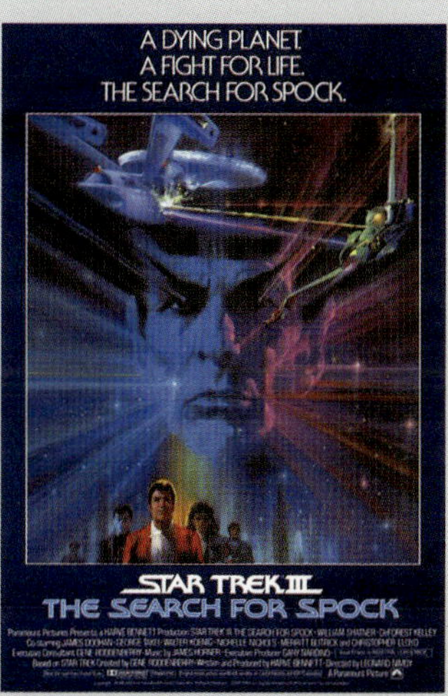

Star Trek III, 1984

Real Genius, 1985

Clueless, 1995

Don't Be a Menace..., 1996

Orange County, 2002

The Holiday, 2006

Made of Honor, 2008

CHAPTER FOUR

O'er her foes
Victorious

In the fall of 1924, a delegation of Occidental students was preparing for a long journey to Hawaii, a trip that was news enough to warrant coverage in the *Los Angeles Times*. The paper reported that the lucky travelers would be chosen for their academic prowess, following strict eligibility requirements established by the faculty.

While Oxy was widely known as a brainy institution, this selection process surely seemed odd to some readers given that the students in question were football players who were scheduled to play against the University of Hawaii. Why would coach Sid Nichols take the best brains on the team instead of the best players on the field?

SKIN THE TIGER

All spin aside, the Oxy players' studies were just as important as the big game. Since the team would be out of class for more than two weeks, it was critical to choose men with enough self-discipline to spend a healthy amount of time with their books. As the *Times* put it, "None of the Tiger heroes will get away without a lot of skull exercise."

Of course, the team ended up getting a lot of exercise in the traditional sense, too. After a rough voyage on the SS *Matsonia*, then a hearty welcome complete with black-and-gold leis and a parade through the streets of downtown Honolulu (filmed by Fox Movietone News), Oxy's 18 football players got down to work. They had only four days to get ready for the game.

Despite Oxy's able team (an "unusually heavy" crew that included tackle Jock Stevens '26, whose hands were large enough to handle a football like a baseball), UH's aggressive plays—rushing and line bucking attacks combined with spot-on forward passes—led to their victory over Occidental, 18-3.

That match, a small disappointment in an otherwise successful season, not only illustrated that familiar Occidental archetype, the scholar-athlete, but also made it a matter of public record.

1894 Occidental banded with Pomona College, the University of Southern California, and Chaffey College to form an intercollegiate athletic conference in Southern California. Oxy's first football players were short on funds for equipment, so they often asked their mothers to sew uniforms fashioned from old clothes.

ABOVE: *Aboard the SS Matsonia, Oxy teammates assume the formation for a photo opportunity.*

LEFT: *A pair of Oxy receivers jockey to catch a pass in the Tigers' 18-3 loss to the University of Hawaii Deans.*

OPPOSITE, TOP: *A UH banner salvaged from the game suggests that the Tigers made it home intact.*

OPPOSITE, BOTTOM: *After arriving in Honolulu on Dec. 2, 1924, the Oxy squad found time to hit the beach (although it's unclear whether the young man on the surfboard is a Tiger or a local).*

1904 Tired of using makeshift equipment, students petitioned the trustees to hire a professional coach and purchase new gear for the gym. They hoped that a $2.50 hike in tuition would be enough to cover the costs.

Let the Games Begin

Occidental has a proud tradition of athletic excellence that stretches back for well over a century. With a handful of other schools, Oxy was one of the founders of intercollegiate competition in Southern California in 1894; one year later, the football team relished its first victory (16-0) over Pomona, the region's oldest rivalry that continues to burn brightly today. The same year, as Southern California's undisputed champions, the Tigers blanked the USC Law School team 10-0.

1911 Coach Joe Pipal joined the coaching staff. After World War I, he left for a time to train Olympic athletes for the newly formed Czechoslovakia. Later, he would lead Oxy's track and field and football teams into the national spotlight.

Early on, Oxy was a fixture on both the regional and national sports scenes—from 1904, when the first of Oxy's almost two dozen Olympians, 1895 graduate Alphonzo E. Bell and 1906 graduate J. Percy Hagerman, placed second in men's doubles and sixth in the long jump, respectively, at the St. Louis games; through the 1920s and 1930s, when Coach Joe Pipal's booming one-liners shaped generations of student-athletes; in the 1940s and 1950s, when Coach Payton Jordan's track and field teams successfully challenged such powers as USC, UCLA, and Stanford and produced national and Olympic champions; in the 1970s and 1980s when women—finally competing on a level playing field—quickly showed what they could do, including a tennis dynasty that claimed a national championship.

ABOVE: Baseball is one of the oldest sports at Oxy, which fielded its first teams in the mid-1890s. Above is the baseball squad from 1919.

OPPOSITE, TOP: Members of the 1906 girls basketball team included captain Vera Brooke 1907 (center), Frances Gordon 1907, Mildred Brookman, Beatrice Fessenden, Marguerite McKalif, and Fairy Means.

OPPOSITE, BOTTOM: Members of Occidental's second football team in 1895-96. In 1913, the Tigers enjoyed their first perfect season; one year later, the Eagle Rock campus hosted its first gridiron contest, where Oxy trounced Redlands, 103-0.

1912

1910 graduate Owen Bird, a sports writer for the *Los Angeles Times*, dubbed the USC football team the Trojans. He had been asked by the university's director of athletics to come up with a new nickname because administrators didn't like being called by the teams' other nicknames, the Methodists and the Wesleyans.

"Occidental College is known for its clean playing. No matter what the result of the Hawaii game may be, we want it to be said that we fought fair and square throughout the contest," Tigers varsity captain Dave Ridderhof '25 told a sportswriter in the hoopla leading up to Oxy's Dec. 6, 1924, contest.

In 1915, Occidental became a founding member of the Southern California Intercollegiate Athletic Conference, pledging itself to avoid what was already seen elsewhere as an over-emphasis on athletics to the detriment of scholarship. "We believe," the SCIAC founding statement says, "it is possible by common effort … to create a mutual athletic life which shall be distinctly and uniquely fine."

Today, with more than one-fourth of the student body participating at the varsity level, athletics remain a vital component of what it means to receive an Occidental education. "Kids at the Division III level are just as competitive as athletes anywhere else, but they know their sport isn't the be-all and end-all," Dixon Farmer '63, who won the 1961 NCAA championship in the 440 hurdles and served as director of athletics from 2000 to 2007, once observed. "They have a sense of balance in their lives, and that's what college athletics should be all about."

1924 J. Clifford Argue '24 competed in the pentathlon at the Olympic games in Paris. Four years later, Nick Carter '25 would run the 1,500-meter race at the Amsterdam games.

Renowned track and field star and 1910 graduate Fred Thomson, who loved to show off in front of his classmates, parlayed that showmanship into a career in show business. Before his early death from tetanus in 1928, he made a name for himself as one of the most popular cowboys of the silent screen.

1938

Oxy won its fourth consecutive conference swimming championships and established its diving record, which would culminate in the winning dives of Sammy Lee '43.

THIS COURT
RESE
FOR VA

A Reputation for Excellence

In 1954, an anonymous Occidental senior wrote to a local sports columnist—a letter the veteran sportswriter called "not only the finest tribute to a living coach I have ever received from an athlete, but the only one of its kind." The student-athlete praised Oxy track coach and athletic director Payton Jordan not for his extraordinary winning record, but for what the student called Jordan's "man-making ability." He wrote that Jordan could "nurture that small spark of self-confidence that is hidden in so many of us, and through his patient way bring out the fire that makes for success in life as well as on the track."

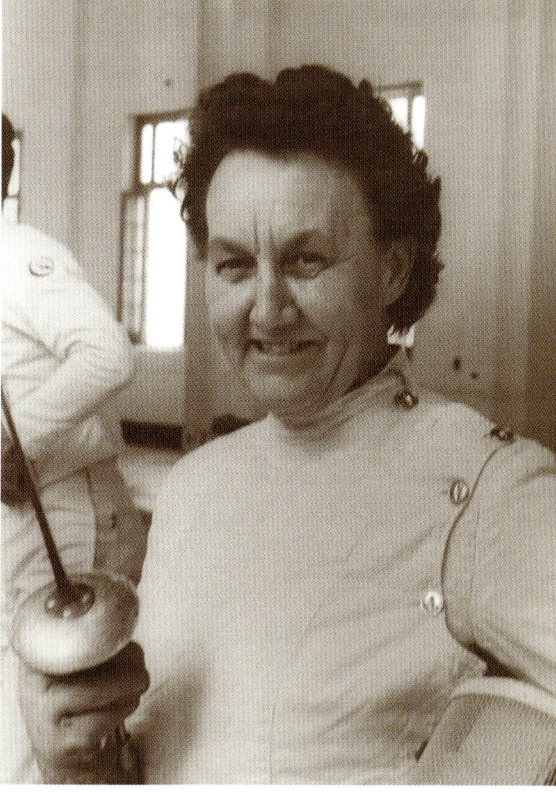

ABOVE: *Fencer Maxine (McMasters) Mitchell '45 competed in three Olympics for the United States: in Melbourne (1956), Rome (1960), and Mexico City (1968).*

LEFT: *Tennis sensation Pat (Henry) Yeomans '38 won the USLTA Girls 18 singles championship in 1935 in Philadelphia after her freshman year. "I played and won singles and doubles at the College Girls Invitational in Boston, representing Oxy in 1936 and 1937," recalls Yeomans.*

OPPOSITE: *Tennis, anyone? Manager Clark MacDonald '38, coach Roy Dennis '33, and members of the 1936 freshman tennis squad, including Bill Kinard, Hugh Golway, William Ward, and John Clark—all from the Class of '40.*

An unbroken string of conference championships and three Olympic athletes under Payton Jordan culminated in the national small college championship in track and field.

Generations of Oxy coaches have been able to find that small spark and fan it into a flame—to the perpetual surprise of sportswriters, who don't associate athletic excellence with a small college that does not offer athletic scholarships and schedules practice to avoid conflicts with classes, rather than the other way around.

Thus it was with the 1948 football team, which capped a perfect 9-0 season on the shoulders of Don Ross '49. The second-string quarterback threw three touchdown passes in the second half to lead Occidental to a stunning, come-from-behind 21-20 victory over heavily favored Colorado A&M in the Raisin Bowl. The Tigers were the only West Coast team to win a New Year's Day game that year, and the only undefeated, untied squad on the West Coast for the season.

LEFT: *Coach Roy Dennis '33 gets a victory lap on the shoulders of Bob Levin '50 following Occidental's Raisin Bowl win.*

ABOVE: *Coach Dennis (back row, far left), assistant coach Al Walz (back row, fourth from right), and members of the Raisin Bowl championship squad. The Tigers—13-point underdogs going into the contest—overcame a 13-point first-half deficit to win the game and secure a permanent place in the annals of Oxy sports history.*

1967

The Oxy Olde Boys Rugby Club played its first season. Oxy's best known rugger, Dave Hodges '90, earned 54 caps over nine years with the Eagles, USA Rugby's men's national team, and played professionally for the Llanelli in Wales for seven years.

Eye of the Tiger
OXY TOPPLES TOREROS AS MILLIONS WATCH

ABOVE: *Move over, Dallas Cowboy Cheerleaders: With the Oxy cheer squad in full effect, a five-person CBS camera crew captured the Tigers' dramatic victory over the University of San Diego. The game was broadcast to 60 percent of the nation.*

OPPOSITE, TOP: *Linebacker Vance Mueller '86 was a fourth-round pick of the Oakland Raiders in 1986, playing 73 games over five seasons for the Silver and Black before sustaining a career-ending knee injury in 1991.*

The University of San Diego was coming off a 9-1 mark in 1981 and a 3-0 start the following season when the Toreros came to Patterson Field to take on Occidental on Oct. 3, 1982. The game was an Oxy first for a number of reasons: It took place on a Sunday; normally staid President Richard Gilman wore a Tiger paw painted on his face; and NFL commentators Dick Stockton and Hank Stram (the latter pulling up to campus in a limousine) were on hand to call the game.

That's because the game was broadcast to 60 percent of the nation's TV markets. When CBS chose the Occidental-USD game as one of four Division III telecasts during week two of the NFL players strike, it rallied the campus around football in a manner seldom seen before. The College, under NCAA rules, received $15,000 for the broadcast. But the exposure for Occidental—and freshman tailback Vance Mueller '86 in particular—proved to be priceless.

First-year coach Dale Widolff's squad rose to the occasion in classic fashion, with Mueller exploding for three touchdowns and 139 total yards in the Tigers' 34-20 rout of the Toreros. The capacity crowd tore down the goalposts, and the media sparked to Oxy. "It had all the ingredients of a second-string screenplay, just the thing to make a producer of B movies drool," Ronald Yates wrote in *The Chicago Tribune*.

Oxy followed that 5-5 season with three consecutive SCIAC championships, and Mueller took a giant leap toward a five-year pro career with the Oakland Raiders. "I talk to kids and I tell them that Oxy was the last place on Earth I ever envisioned going, and it turned out to be the best place for me," Mueller (who missed out on a gridiron scholarship with Oklahoma following a season-ending injury as a high school senior) told *Los Angeles Times* writer Jerry Crowe in 2007, on the game's 25th anniversary. "I think sometimes you just have to be open to going where the adventure takes you."

Playing for Keeps

While the 1931-32 Occidental student handbook lists a "well-rounded program of sports" for women, including "hockey, basketball, baseball, swimming, tennis, handball, archery, fencing, and horseshoes," the modern era of women's athletics began in 1961, when coaches from five other Southern California schools set up leagues in four sports.

But those days before Title IX—the landmark 1972 legislation that prohibits sex discrimination in educational institutions receiving federal funds—were not easy for the female student-athlete. "We got the gym three days a week at lunch, and that was our practice time," recalls Janet McCreery '67, who played basketball and volleyball at Occidental. Often lacking uniforms, women athletes had to spray-paint their jersey numbers on what McCreery calls "stupid one-piece jumpsuits."

ABOVE: *Barbara Rush, Alice McDowell, and Libby Young—all from the Class of '37—ride over the bridle path at Arroyo Stables near the Oxy campus.*

RIGHT: *Dorothy Alice Burson '47 takes aim while her fellow archery students await their turns in April 1946.*

OPPOSITE, TOP LEFT: *Members of the women's tennis team in 1982-83: (front row, l-r) Amy Marcus '84, Jean Marie Sanders '84, and Diana Driscoll '87; (middle row) Tina Martin '85, Suzanne Davies '85, Yvonne Orozco '84, Lisa Gray '85, and Caroline Chen '86; (back row) coach Lynn Pacala, Lee Rutter '86, Jean Gilliland '83, Margie Goodspeed '85, Wendy Antisdel '84, and assistant coach Craig Witcher.*

OPPOSITE, TOP RIGHT: *Garnett Engen '84 puts down a spike against two La Verne defenders in 1983.*

1968

Chuck Smith '70 placed fifth in the 200-meter dash at the Mexico City Olympics. He had never competed until he was discovered during his junior year, earning him the nickname "the Cinderella Athlete."

By the time the SCIAC began sponsoring women's play in 1976, the uniforms improved—and success was soon to follow. The Tigers ended the 1981-82 season with four conference championships—in cross country, tennis, track, and volleyball—as well as two second-place finishes in two other sports. The track team, coached by Bill Harvey '67, went undefeated in conference meets, winning by an unprecedented point spread, while women's volleyball earned a conference title for the sixth consecutive year.

But the real story was women's tennis, which had just become an NCAA-sanctioned sport that year. After going a perfect 10-0 at the conference championship, Oxy women went on to win the team competition at the NCAA Division III nationals.

Not bad for a single year.

ABOVE: *Track and field teammates Angelique Green '87, Noella Allan '86, Kim Donaldson '86, and Mary Kempner '86.*

1972 Janet McCreery '67 organized a walkout of female coaches in the school district in which she worked after the district failed to respond promptly to the passage of federal legislation prohibiting sex discrimination in educational institutions receiving federal funds.

Excellence Endures

ABOVE: *Track coach Joseph A. Pipal and Claude Kilday '38, "the one-man track team."*

OPPOSITE PAGE *(clockwise from top left): Payton Jordan (crouched, right) offers a few pointers to members of the 1949 freshman track squad; John Barnes '52 runs the 880 in the 1951 NCAA meet in Seattle; teammates Phil Schlegel '52, Bill Cotrel '51, Barnes, Walt McKibben '52, Bill Parker '50, and Coach Jordan leave for the Drake Relays in April 1950; Oxy and USC runners come down to the wire in a 1962 meet; and Ted Ruprecht '51 breaks the tape in the relay against Stanford on April 20, 1951.*

The truth is, you can take almost any season in Occidental's history and compile similar examples of excellence. Some, like the dominance of the men's track team through the 1960s, are nothing short of legendary. By 1932, Coach Joe Pipal had led the track team to five consecutive championship victories; for years afterward, his famous line, "Ye gods, man, get those knees up!" would reverberate in the memories of countless alumni. (And as his struggling protégés would come staggering around the final turn, Pipal would roar, in a voice that stopped traffic over on York Boulevard: "Come on, men, start your sprints!")

1979 *Track and Field News* reported that 37 Oxy men had ranked nationally in the sport since 1963. During that time, 25 also earned world rankings.

OXY
FROSH
OXY
FROSH
OXY
FROSH
TWA

Sammy Lee '43 was an "old man" of 28 when he won the first of two gold medals in diving at the Olympics in 1948.

Soon after came Payton Jordan, who arrived at Occidental in 1946 as a 29-year-old head coach following a stint in the Navy in World War II. During his decade at Oxy, his teams competed against the best in the country, winning 10 conference championships, an NAIA national title in 1956, and two top-five finishes in the NCAA championships in 1951 and 1952. His athletes set a world record in the distance medley relay, won four individual NCAA championships, and competed in the 1952 Olympics, with Bob McMillen '53 bringing home a silver medal in the 1,500-meter run.

At those same games in Helsinki, diver Sammy Lee '43 scored his second gold medal off the 10-meter board, repeating his Olympics success from the London games in 1948.

1981 Sue Bethanis '82, captain of the volleyball team, led her players to a third-place finish in the NCAA Division III national championships.

While still an undergraduate at Oxy, Lee came in first place at the Amateur Athletic Union meet in 1942 in the 3- and 10-meter events. The Korean-American athlete had trained hard for that win, squeezing in half-hour workouts whenever he had downtime during the chemistry labs required for his pre-med studies. He also put in off-campus training sessions with his coach, Jim Ryan, a 6-foot-4, 275-pound bull of a man who insisted that the 5-foot-2 Lee practice diving in a sandpit in Ryan's backyard instead of a pool. However unconventional his training, it yielded results.

McMillen and Lee weren't the only Olympic medalists of that era with Oxy in their blood. After winning a bronze in the 110-meter hurdles in the 1948 Summer Olympics, Craig Dixon '48 blazed through every race he entered the following year, notching 59 consecutive hurdle victories, including national crowns in both the NCAA and AAU high and low hurdles. And at the 1956 Melbourne Games, two of the three medalists in the pole vault had ties to the College—Bob Gutowski '58 (silver) and Greek-born George Roubanis (bronze), who spent a single year at Oxy in 1955 before transferring to UCLA.

ABOVE: *Craig Dixon '48 took home the bronze in the 110-meter hurdles at the 1948 Summer Olympics in London.*

BELOW: *Pole vaulter Bob Gutowski '58 won a silver medal at the 1956 Summer Olympics in Melbourne, Australia.*

OPPOSITE, TOP LEFT: *Coach Kevin McNair (front row, center) and members of the 1977 Division III national champion men's cross country team: All-America picks Steve Bitterly (front, left) and Tom Colley '78 (front, right); (back row, l-r) Gil Acedo '78, Mike Bradner '80, Phil Sweeney '78, Eric Gulve '80, and Bob Kyczko '80. Occidental also won the track and field nationals in spring 1978.*

OPPOSITE, TOP RIGHT: *An unidentified lacrosse player from a club team in the 1970s.*

OPPOSITE, BOTTOM: *Distance runner Pam Morris '79 was Oxy's first national class women's track athlete, participating in the Olympic trials in 1980.*

TOP LEFT: *Considered by many to be the greatest coach in Occidental baseball history, Grant Dunlap '46 (back row, left, with his 1976 squad) had a career record of 525-311-8 while coaching 10 conference championship teams between 1954 and 1984.*

BOTTOM LEFT: *A relative late-comer to golf, Olin Browne '81 joined the Oxy links team as a sophomore and gradually moved up to the No. 1 player. He won the first of his three PGA victories to date in July 1998, at the Canon Greater Hartford Open, and scored his biggest payday to date ($990,000) by winning the 2005 Deutsche Bank Championship.*

1984

Patterson Field was overhauled in preparation for the Olympics. $1.5 million was pumped into the renovation of the field, including new training facilities and bleachers.

Kemp to Mora: A Winning Combo

BELOW, LEFT: In two seasons as quarterback for the Tigers, Jack Kemp '57 led Oxy to a 9-8 mark. A 17th-round draft pick by the Detroit Lions in 1957, his pro career took off in 1960 with the formation of the American Football League.

BELOW, RIGHT: Kemp stumps for the Republican Party as the GOP's vice presidential candidate in 1996.

Oxy roommates and 1957 classmates Jack Kemp and Jim Mora were All-SCIAC teammates and team co-captains on an Oxy football squad that only went 3-6 their senior year—but their gridiron careers were anything but over.

Playing quarterback for the Tigers, Kemp was the third-ranked small-college quarterback in the nation as a senior and was drafted by the Detroit Lions. He played 13 years as a pro, winning MVP honors in the American Football League in 1965 for the Buffalo Bills, before turning to politics.

After three years as a starter for Occidental at tight end and defensive end, Mora played for base teams at Quantico, Va., and Camp Lejeune, N.C., as a Marine, butting heads with college squads such as Holy Cross and Boston College. When his service was up, Mora returned to Los Angeles without a job—and new Occidental head coach Vic Schwenk hired Mora as an assistant coach for the Tigers. Four years later, at age 29, he became head coach.

By the late 1980s, both players were at the top of their respective games. Kemp, a nine-term U.S. Congressman representing western New York, sought the Republican nomination for president in 1988. Mora, meanwhile, rose through the college and pro ranks (including a pair of United States Football League championships) to become an NFL head coach, compiling a 125-112 record over 11 seasons with the New Orleans Saints and four more with the Indianapolis Colts.

Half a century after wearing a Tigers football jersey, Kemp—who served as Health, Education, and Welfare secretary under President George H.W. Bush and graced the 1996 Republican presidential ticket as Sen. Bob Dole's running mate—frequently offers commentary on politics on cable news channels. Meanwhile, Mora—who won a new generation of fans through a Coors Light ad incorporating old footage from a legendary press conference about the playoffs—is an analyst for the NFL Network.

ABOVE: *Oxy's all-time No. 2 scorer, Finn Rebassoo '03 powered the Tigers to an undefeated regular season in the SCIAC, a conference-first berth in NCAA Division III basketball's Elite Eight, and a career-best 25-3 season for coach Brian Newhall '83.*

RIGHT: *(Clockwise from top left) Seniors Song Cun, Chase Young, Jelani Young, Joey Cabarrus, Finn Rebassoo, Tyler Rogers, and Gavin Keohane—all members of the Class of 2003—formed the nucleus of the winningest Tigers squad ever.*

The women's water polo team won the Collegiate III championship in a match that went into double overtime, earning the College's first national title in 18 years.

LEFT: *After the buzzer sounded in the Tigers' 80-61 Division III playoff victory over the Spartans—sending Occidental to the Sweet 16—the Rush Gym floor was flooded with fans, family, cheerleaders, and players (including Jefani Kelly '03, foreground).*

BELOW: *Ending an 18-year drought of national titles, the women's water polo team won the Division III championship on May 7, 2000, in a double-overtime thriller over Claremont-Mudd-Scripps. Goalie Jackie Provost '02 was named tourney MVP and SCIAC player of the year.*

New Century, Same Excellence

Since the turn of the century, Occidental's athletics program has excelled in ways that would bring smiles to the giants of years gone by—from Pipal and Jordan to the late Dennis Fosdick, who saw his women's water polo squad to a Division III championship in 2000, then died of cancer in 2003.

Brian Newhall '83—who stepped up from the assistant ranks to coach his alma mater's basketball team in 1988—has enjoyed the greatest success of his storied career in the new millennium. His 2002-03 Tigers ran the boards in the SCIAC to go 16-0 en route to a 25-3 record and raising the profile of SCIAC basketball with a remarkable run to the Elite Eight.

2001

Meaghan Dunne '01 became the captain of both the women's and men's cross country teams when there were no returning men to assume the leadership role.

Going into the 2008 season, Dale Widolff ranked ninth among winningest active football coaches in Division III. From 2004 to 2007, his Tigers ran up an unprecedented 32-game regular-season winning streak that included three conference championships, an Elite Eight berth (in 2004), and a pair of Sweet 16 finishes. The key to the Tigers' offense was quarterback Andy Collins '07, a native of Yakima, Wash., who spurned a scholarship offer from the University of Oregon and found out about Oxy while sifting through a box of old recruiting letters. "When times were toughest, Andy brought his game to another level," Widolff said in 2006. "In all my years of coaching, I've never seen a student-athlete have as big an impact on a team's success."

LEFT: *Wide receiver Josh Jones '06 caught two TDs during the first half of the Tigers' 28-14 victory over Willamette University in 2005—Occidental's first postseason win in 20 years. One week later, the Tigers reached Division III football's Elite Eight with a 42-40 upset of Concordia-Moorhead of Minnesota.*

TOP: *The Tigers raise high the Shoes trophy—a pair of bronze football shoes that have gone to the victor of the Oxy-Whittier game since 1946.*

ABOVE: *Since 1941, the Drum has been the centerpiece of the annual football contest between Occidental and its oldest rival, Pomona.*

OPPOSITE: *Quarterback Andy Collins '07 guided the Tigers to a 26-0 regular-season mark over three years at the helm.*

2004 Shawn Lawson-Cummings '86, vice president of international licensing and sponsorships for Major League Baseball, was named one of the 101 most influential minorities in sports by *Sports Illustrated* in its June 28 issue. Lawson-Cummings (No. 26) was a two-time Division III national heptathlon champion while in college.

In 2007, identical twins Jon and Robert Dohring '08 gave Occidental sports enthusiasts plenty to talk about. Dedicated gymnasts turned divers once they got to college, Jon and Robert finished first and second, respectively, in the 1- and 3-meter events at the NCAA Division III swimming and diving nationals. "I certainly didn't expect to make it to nationals in my four years, let alone win," says Jon, whose victories came 65 years after Sammy Lee's 3-meter and 10-meter triumphs at the National AAU swim meet.

You can trace a clear line of excellence from 1907 graduate Clarence Spaulding—Glee Club member, student body president, catcher and outfielder on the championship 1906 baseball team, and Oxy's first Rhodes Scholar—to the Dohrings. But similar stories abound of versatile, talented athletes who remain committed to both quality education and sportsmanship. That's what the presidents of Occidental, Caltech, Pomona, Redlands, and Whittier had in mind when they banded together in 1915 to create something distinctly and uniquely fine—a proud legacy that Oxy scholar-athletes carry on today.

2008

The women's basketball team claims its first conference championship since 1980, setting a new record for wins in a season (20).

LEFT/ABOVE: *In 2007-08, guards Stacie Roshon '08, left, and Brianne Brown '09, above, led Oxy women's basketball to its first SCIAC crown in 28 years.*

BELOW LEFT: *A mud-covered Alex Ramon '08 (178) finished 142nd in the NCAA Division III Championships following the Oxy cross country squad's 39th SCIAC title in 2006— the team's first since 1995.*

OPPOSITE: *Identical twins Jon and Robert Dohring—members of the Class of '08—finished first and second, respectively, in the 1- and 3-meter competitions at the NCAA Division III swimming and diving nationals in March 2007.*

COMMENCEMENT.